Basic Legal English

By KagKeun Yu
InHee Kwon

Published by
SUN MOON UNIVERSITY

Contents

Chapter 4. Rights and Duties

Chapter 5. Constitutional Law

Chapter 6. Law of Prohibition on Gender Discrimination

Chapter 7. Crime and Criminal Law

Chapter 8. Administrative Law

Chapter 9. Employment Relations

Chapter 10. Labor Union

Chapter 11. Intellectual Property

Chapter 12. The Marriage Institution

Chapter 13. *De Facto* Marriage and Divorce

Chapter 14. International Law

Preface

This book is designed to introduce basic legal English to first year law students and laymen who are interested in both law and English. Amidst globalization and internationalization, students and businessmen everywhere are eager to study English. Law is the philosophy, history and soul of a society. Furthermore, law is a bundle of virtues for the society to keep and protect. Therefore, the study of legal English for beginners is challenging and yet exciting and fruitful. Frankly speaking, even we authors were afraid and resistant to write this book at the beginning. To study complicated law in English is like undergoing a double torture. However, at the same time, we believe that it is worth it to try to write this kind of book since both law and English are indispensable in this current age.

This book is unique in the sense that the Korean legal system is introduced in English. In order to meet the demand for a textbook of a one-semester course for beginners, this book has been arranged so that basic law can be very easily understood. We tried to include all of the subjects necessary to the mastery of basic law. The content of the book includes the concept of law, explaining why all people need to follow law for the protection of justice. Fundamental rights are mainly introduced in the Constitution, and criminal law and administrative law are discussed briefly. As far as civil law is concerned, only family law is explained.

One of us, Kag-Keun Yu, who has experience in studying abroad in Japan felt that writing basic legal English textbook was nonsense. But the fact that there are few resources available for students to easily understand basic legal English became the motivation to face this challenge. Although there are introductory materials which would allow students to become familiar with American law, no legal English book with a focus on the Korean legal system is available so far. Even though our other author, In-Hee Kwon, had studied in the United States for several years, we anticipate that there are limits to our English expressions in this book. Also, the amount of information that can be digested in only one semester is quite limited, and some sections of this book may be too short to understand clearly. So, we promise better material hereafter will come.

Authors greatly appreciate Yong-Hyob Shin (student in Ph. D. course) for his help in editing and proofreading the English rough draft. Also, we thank Harmony Becker, who made great efforts as editorial supervisor, and to all those at Sun Moon University who gladly gave their permission for us to write this book, even under the difficult publishing circumstances. Thank you all from the bottom of our heart!

August 25, 2011

Kag-Keun Yu and In-Hee Kwon

References

- Arthur R. Miller and Michael H. Davis, Intellectual Property, 4th Edition, West Group, 2007
- Bongsoo Jung, Korean Labor Law Bible, Jungang Keyngjae, 2006
- Douglas L. Leslie, Labor Law, Nuecsell, 1992
- Gould, William B, A Primer on American Labor Law, waseda,1994
- Jay M. Feinman, Law 101, 3rd Edition, Oxford University Press, 2010
- Moritoshi Fukuda, translated by Deok-Young Park, American Law and Legal English, Pakyoungsa, 2009
- Rhim & Lee's Dictionary of Law, Bobmunsa, 2007
- Robert P. Merges, Peter S. Menell and Mark A. Lemley, Intellectual Property in the New Technological Age, 3rd Edition, Aspen Publishes, 2003
- Seong-Jae Moon et al., Understanding of Modern Law, 2nd Edition, Bobmunsa, 2011
- Steven H. Gifis, Dictionary of Legal Terms, BARRON`S, 1998

Chapter 1 The Concept of Law

Section 1. What is Law?

Ⅰ. The concept of law

It is difficult to define precisely the concept of law. The meaning of the law differs by country and region. For example, in the Orient, the law has been traditionally regarded as 'rules to pursue virtue of the society and to enforce fairness or equity'. However, in the Occident, the law has been considered as 'rules to enforce justice', meaning both rightness and right. The meaning of the law depends on inherited culture and history. Therefore, it is better to understand the law by its characteristics and function as a social standard, not by its definition.

Ⅱ. The characteristics of law

1. Law is a standard

A human being who lives in a society is ruled by the law of the society - the standard that rules human life in a community. Furthermore, a human being who lives in nature is ruled by the law of nature. A human being is ruled thus by both social and natural principles.

Social principles require the rational restriction of both a person's mind and conduct. Together with morality, religion, and custom, law is necessary to social life. Namely, the saying, "Where there is society, there is law" means that if the society exists, the law exists. It also means that law must exist only within society.

2. Law is a social standard

The law as a social standard has a function to restrain any man in order to observe community order. In ancient society, a single comprehensive social standard which encompasses all norms, such as law, morality, religion, custom, etc., sufficiently ruled the society with order. But as human history has made progress and social life has become more complicated, the social standard has also been divided into various types of standards, such as law, morality, religion, custom, etc. Among them, in modern times, the law has been distinguished as separate from the others - especially from morality. Here the law has become an independent social standard, one which has assumed an important role in maintaining order in society.

3. Law is a behavioral standard

The object of the law is human behavior or conduct. Conduct, meaning 'a physical behavior of a human being with intention', is the object of the law, and mere desire without external expression is not. The law is the standard used to distinguish between what is valuable and what is not valuable to society. Thus, the law is a barometer that decides what should be done and what should not be done. In this sense, the law is a behavioral standard which orders that one "MUST

DO" or "MUST NOT DO" a certain action. In other words, the law enforces people to do what they are ordered to do.

4. Law is a mandatory standard

The law is a mandatory standard in the sense that its restraints are imposed on illegal conduct to keep order in society. For example, the provision of "A person who kills another person shall be sentenced to death, life imprisonment, or more than five years' imprisonment." (Article 250 Clause 1 in Criminal Act) implies that restraint would be imposed on the conduct that violates the clause, "Don't kill another person". The law is enforced by the state's power, and restraints will be imposed on any violation.

The law is a mandatory standard in order to guarantee its effectiveness. As a result, it is to preserve the predictability and stability of the law by informing that restraints will be imposed on people for illegal conduct. In that the law is approved by the nation and enforced by the state power, the law is distinguished from other social standards such as morality and religion, which are practiced by personal conscience.

Section 2. Law and Social Standards

Ⅰ. How does the law differ from other social standards?

The law governs human life along with other social standards such as morality, religion, and custom. In ancient days, these norms were combined together to be considered one single social standard. But they have been separated into independent standards due to the development of society and the complexity of human life. And, as a result, each has become its own distinctive social standard, respectively pursuing distinctive values from independent positions. However, in modern society, these social norms are correlated with each other, instead of being divided completely. It is hard to separate law from other social standards since the law must contain humanity as well as rationality to rule the society.

1. Law and morality

Morality is a social norm which pursues good and forbids evil. Therefore, it is necessary to keeping social order, along with the law. However, morality is different from the law in many aspects, and understanding the difference is important to grasp a clear understanding of the law. There are various opinions presented by several legal experts.

Fig.1.1. Law and morality

* Law and morality have an mseperable relation and work in cooperation

(1) Externality and internality

While the law regulates a person's external conduct, morality regulates one's internal counterparts, such as internal mind or conscience. Thus, the internality of morality is distinguished from the externality of the law. As goes the saying, "Nobody shall be punished for thought by the law", legal punishment is not allowed for a person's internal thought. However, it is morally wrong to desire to steal another person's possession. But there are also other trends in which legal judgment aims at not only exterior action but also interior mind, and moral evaluation aims at outward action as well as inward mind.

(2) Heteronomy and autonomy

The law is a heteronomous standard enforced by society. Morality is an autonomous standard in alignment with the conscience. However, it seems that people have already observed the law autonomously even before the law has been enacted because many articles in Criminal Act have been regulated in such a way that one "MUST NOT DO" a certain act. Morality is also heteronomous in the sense that it is required by others to observe. Thus, it is hard to distinguish between the law and the morality only by the heteronomy-autonomy test, as both have close relations with each other.

(3) Forcibleness and forcelessness

There is another point of view to distinguish between the law and the morality. Law is distinguished from morality in that while the former is a standard executed by a forcible power, the latter is a standard executed by a forceless power like the conscience. However, it is true that there are also provisions with little to no forcibleness. Therefore, the only way to distinguish between law and morality is only by the test that law has forcibleness but morality does not. What is certain is that the law has a forcible effect in that it does direct most of its attention to external conduct, while the morality does not in that it directs most of its attention only to internal conscience. In this regard, law and morality are different. That is to say, both are different in that the law can take an external forcible measure based on the state's power, while the morality can take an internal forcible restraint through only mental or psychological process.

As stated until now, even though both have many differences, in some cases, to distinguish between law and morality is very hard. In other words, the distinction between law and morality is possible in conception, but it is not easy to distinguish one from the other in that both of them together constitute behavioral standards of social life in a community. Law and morality cannot be isolated from each other and thus can be merely distinguished.

2. Law and religion

(1) Religion also restrains human beings as law does.

What relation does law have to religion? In ancient society, law and religion were not separated from each other but ruled society as one united standard. For example, the Ten Commandments and the Five Buddhist Commandments of the Silla Dynasty were observed not only as rules of religion, but also as legal regulations.

However, not all rules of religion are legal, and not all of legal regulations are religious. The rule of religion must be observed to worship God or the Almighty in a sacred way. On the other hand, the law is enforced by the state's power to rule the nonspiritual civil world.

Fig.1.2. Law and Religion

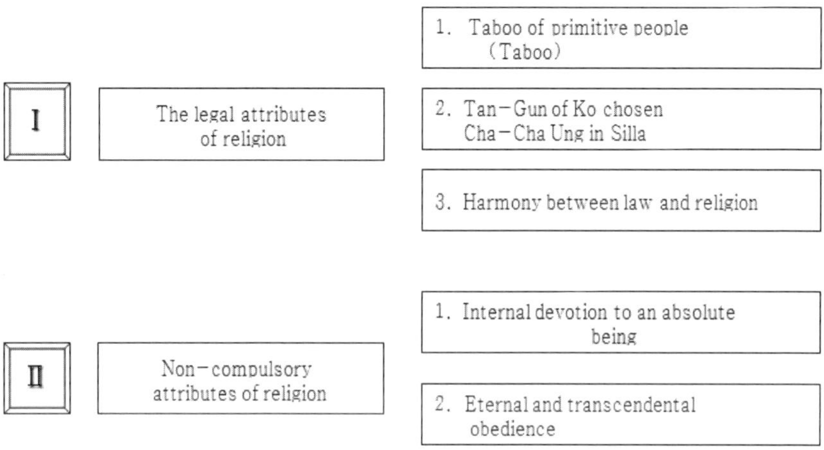

※ Through the separation of church and state, secular and spiritual matters are separated.

(2) Religion is not mandatory.

The law is enacted, practiced, and enforced by the state's power. However, religion is the divine worship of God. In other words, law rules people's external conduct while religion calls for people's internal belief. Although religion also influences people's external conduct, it is distinguished from law in that it is intrinsically spiritual.

Therefore, law and religion are distinguished from each other in the aspect of both foundations and forcibleness. A lawyer thus pursues the ideas of law; a religious believer, on the other hand, pursues perpetuity and tranquillity of mind.

3. Law and custom

It is not easy to conceptually distinguish between law and custom. It may be somewhat possible to distinguish in the sense that law is enacted artificially, but custom is adopted spontaneously. However, it is impossible to think of making laws without consideration of traditional custom. Both law and custom are all the same in that they govern social life. Nonetheless, the former is compelled by the state's power, while the latter is respected by personal perception of tradition.

Fig.1.3. Law and Customs

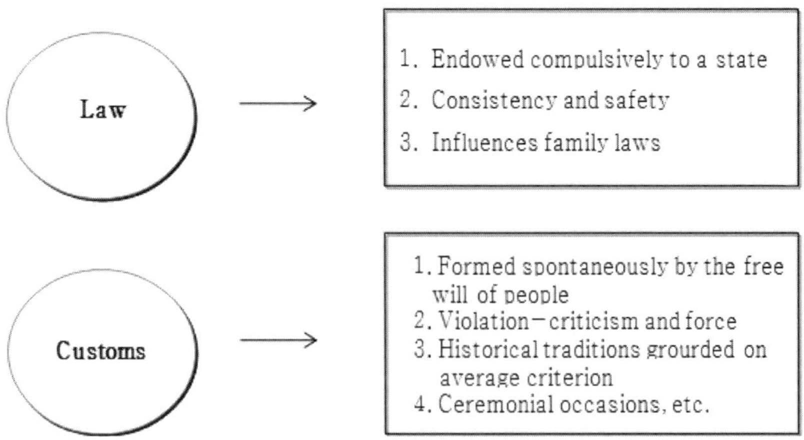

Custom is established spontaneously by family, race, or society, and formed naturally and historically. When a custom is not observed, then criticism is allowed but its enforcement is not.

Section 3. The Objective of Law

1. Justice

Justice is the virtue that should be observed rationally. Justice is also one of the general and universal principles of the world which ought to be pursued ideally.

Aristotle divided the concept of justice into two types - special justice general justice and special justice. He then divided the latter into two types - average justice and distributive justice. General justice honors mutual respect for personal rights in a community and obliges civic duty to follow the general principles of the community.

Average justice adjusts individual interests for unbiased and harmonized common interests. It aims at absolute equality by the principle of "treating equals equally and unequals unequally" in order to achieve balance of the community. Distributive justice focuses on apportioning respect, goods, and other rewards in proportion to one's ability and contribution.

In general, justice means equality. But it does not mean all people should be treated exactly the same. It only means the equality of standards themselves, under which everyone is treated unequally in proportion to one's ability and contribution. In turn, it means proportional equality. Thus, distributive justice is regarded as fundamental and average justice is deemed to be only one of the applications of the distributive justice.

2. Proper objectivity

Proper objectivity is the appropriateness of law for a purpose. In other words, it requires that a law must be enacted and implemented properly according to its function and objectivity. While justice leads to the generalization of law, proper objectivity induces the concreteness and individualization of law.

3. Legal stability

Due to legal stability, people are able to manage calm and steady lawful lives. The prerequisite for legal stability requires the following: firstly, the contents of the law should be clear. Secondly, law should not be amended easily. Thirdly, law should be effective. And lastly, law should be appropriate for people's recognition.

Section 4. The Function of Law

The law is a social institution created by society and as such, its social roles are very important. The law should fulfill its functions well in order to keep social vitality. While the objective of law is to provide an internal and ideological standard of society, the function of law is to solve external and realistic problems of society.

The function of law is to realize the objective of law through its implementation. The objective of law has correlations with the function of law.

1. The function of maintaining social order

The law is a mandatory standard which builds and maintains social order. Regulations of law are enforced to maintain social order and stability. Also, the law consists of rules which regulate person-to-person relations as well as person-to-organization relations in communal life. In addition, the law protects personal rights of liberty and equality.

2. The function of regulation

To realize its objectives, law regulates certain personal conduct with authorization by ordering, compelling, and forbidding. Authorized constraints are imposed on the violation of law. Consequently, law controls social order and realizes the national objective. As such, law has roles to maintain social order and induce social progress.

3. The function of evaluating

Law has the function of evaluating lawful and unlawful conducts, since law is a behavioral standard of society. Law has the objective of social justice, and people observe the law with respect. Thus, the law presents an exemplary model for personal conduct for people to follow in order to lead a peaceful life.

Chapter 2 The Classification of law

Section1. The Existential Type of Law

Ⅰ. The codified law (*lex scripta*)

1. The concept of the codified law

Codified law is written law and is also called by statutory law. Codified law is an ordered grouping of legal principles enacted into law by a state legislature. It is also a regulation enacted by local governments with authority. Countries having the civil law system have codified laws as sources of law and exceptionally accept unwritten laws supplementarily. Constitutional law, statutory law (act), administrative decree, administrative regulation (rule), and treaty exist as codified laws in Korea.

Fig.2.1. The classification of law

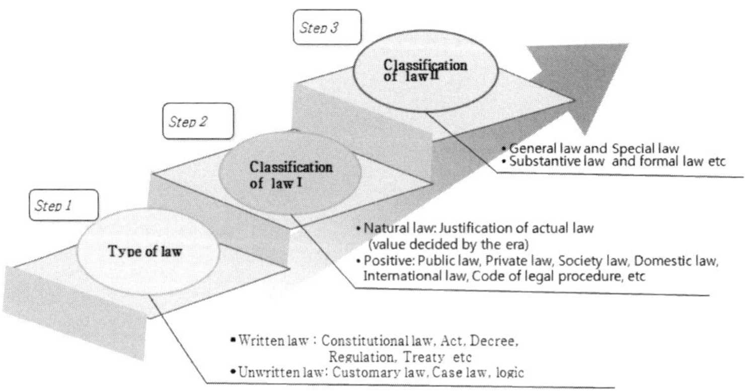

2. The classification of codified law

(1) Constitutional law

Constitutional law is a body of law dealing with governmental structure, distribution and exercise of government power, and the fundamental rights of citizens. Conceptually, constitutional laws can be divided into two categories - the formal constitutional law and the substantive constitutional law. The former means "the constitution" as a statute law type, while the latter does not require that it should be always "the Constitution". The examples of the latter are National Assembly Act, Political Parties Act, Constitutional Court Act, Board of Audit and Inspection Act, Petition Act, and so on.

(2) Acts

Acts are divided into two conceptional categories - acts in a broad sense and acts in a limited sense. The former means the law as a general norm, including both written and unwritten types. The latter means only the statutory law that the National Assembly has enacted, and it is called the 'formal sense of the law'. This formal sense of the law is a law that defines the constitution: A law in violation of the constitution will be declared invalid and will not be enforced. Likewise, an administrative decree or a regulation also shall not be against the related act because it is the lower rank in legal hierarchy. But there are no relations of dominance between acts themselves.

When there are conflicts between articles of acts, generally a new act is superior to an old act and a special act dominates a general act.

(3) Decree

A decree is a statutory law especially enacted by an administrative government organization other than the state legislature. In legal hierarchy, a decree is located under an act; it is not able to effectuate or invalidate either the constitution or an act. However, decrees enacted by the President in emergencies are exceptions.

According to the purpose of legislation, decrees are distinguished into two types - executable order and delegated order. An executable order is a decree that is established to execute orders of superior authorities, thus it is generally known as an "enforcement decree" or an "enforcement regulation".

(4) Regulation (Rule)

A regulation (rule) is a statutory law enacted by a constitutional institution. It must be legislated in compliance with acts established by the National Assembly or other constitutional institutions. There are also administrative rules which are established to regulate internal orders of administrative organizations and special authoritative relations. Administrative rules are named generally as regulations (rules), directives, orders, established rules, notices, provisions and so on.

(5) Treaty

A treaty is an expressed agreement under international law by contracting parties, namely sovereign states and international organizations. There are several types of agreements, such as (international) agreements, convention, protocol, declaration, charter, and consent. Regardless of terminology used, there is no difference in legal effects; a treaty binds its members' conduct. To conclude a treaty, firstly, delegates from countries or international organizations draw up a treaty draft and sign it. Then, the National Assembly give consent to the treaty and the Present finally ratifies it. Treaties duly concluded and announced under the Constitution, as well as generally recognized rules of international law, shall have the same effect as the domestic laws.

Ⅱ. Unwritten law (*lex non scripta*)

1. The concept of unwritten law

Unwritten law is law established by customs, conventions, and judicial decisions, as distinguished from the enactments of orders or decrees in writing by the legislature.

2. The classification of unwritten law

(1) Customary law

Customary law is the established pattern of behavior that can be objectively verified as a law within society. Customary law is the social custom generally accepted as a legal standard with the conviction that the court previously confirmed. To be a customary law, observed custom should be repeated many times and finally accepted with strong conviction as a source of law (opinion juris) among members of society. The customary law should have all the values and functions of law.

The article 106 of the Civil Act provides "If there is a custom which differs from any provisions of the Act or subordinate statutes which are not concerned with good morals or other social order, and if the intention of the parties to a juristic act is not clear, such custom shall prevail." and thus it distinguishes de facto custom from customary law in the article 1 of the Civil Act.

A custom can be a customary law where :

① a certain customary practice has existed and been observed for a long time, and

② the relevant parties consider it to be law (opinio juris), and

③ the custom should not be against good morals and other social order, and

④ the custom should be admitted by the legal provisions or concerned with no legal provisions.

In general, only subsidiary effect can be allowed for customary law. That is, customary law is supplementary to statutory law. However, there are opinions that customary law should also be admitted to have equal effect to statutory law.

(2) Case law (Judicial decision)

Case law is a law that has been established and obtained with what is called de facto binding force by following decisions made by judges in earlier cases. Because legislation cannot always keep up with the rapid development of society, there occurs a gap between enacted law and reality. Therefore, judicial decisions fill the gap supplementarily and temporarily.

Judicial decisions are not allowed to be enforced legally. Nonetheless, there are opinions being raised that a judicial decision, repeated many times over a period of time, is already a customary law.

As a matter of fact, the court is making judicial decisions according to the precedents, especially those of the higher court. And if a court did not follow the precedents of the higher court, its judgment is likely to be reversed by the higher court. Judicial decisions of the Supreme Court in particular would not be changed easily in order to keep legal unity and stability. Therefore, a lower court has a tendency to follow the precedents of the Supreme Court. And, as a result, it is true that the judicial decision (of the Supreme Court) has a de facto binding force.

(3) Sound reasoning

Sound reasoning accepted as a supplementary source of law complies with the nature or logic of things. It is expressed as the name of justice, equity, common sense, good faith, and so on. Sound reasoning is changeable according to social and historical conditions, and has close relation to morality. Even though sound reasoning is not enforced as a law, it is applied by the court. Article 1 of the Civil Act recognizes sound reasoning as a source of unwritten law by providing that if no provisions apply to certain civil affairs in the Act, and if no applicable customary law exists, sounding reasoning shall apply. Thus, it works as not only a judicial standing rule but also a standard of legal interpretation of provisions or contracts.

Section 2. The Classification of Law

1. Natural law and positive law

A natural law has been described as a law of which content is set by nature, not by human's empirical basis and is thus ideal, universal, and everlasting in spite of time and place. A natural law is a supra-legal norm intuitively recognizable by rational reason and filled with the idea of justice. Thus, a natural law is law that should be observed in every law of a nation, and is not a law enacted by the nation.

A positive law is defined as a law which applies at a certain time (present or past) at a certain place based on all empirical and historical facts. In this sense, it is distinguished from an eternal and unchanging natural law. Therefore, a positive law is law that is unavoidably limited by historical and empirical facts in real society and is only recognized by the empirical factors which are created and changed artificially.

2. General law and special law

A general law is a law which is applied universally to people without any restriction on the person, the place or the area. A special law, on the contrary, is applied to only some specific occupational clusters or limited areas of living. In other words, it is called a special law if a law is only applied to a certain person, a certain place or a certain area. In general, where there is a special law (and where there is a general law as well), the special law can be applied by priority. Furthermore, a general law can be applied only where there is no special law. This is the principle of what is called the 'special law's priority'.

3. Public law and private law

There are opposing theories for the criteria of distinctions between public and private laws. (1) The Benefit Approach is the theory that a public law pursues public interests, while a private law pursues private interests. (2) The Attribute Approach is the theory that a public law regulates unequal relations, but a private law regulates equal relations. (3) The Agent Approach is the theory that a public law concerns interrelations between the public powers such as the state and public institutions, or relations between the public power and private citizens, whereas a private law concerns interactions between private citizens, including the state as a private individual.

4. Domestic law and international law

A domestic law is a law that has been established and enforced by a state, the unitary sovereignty. A domestic law mainly concerns the internal relations of a state. That is to say, it rules over the relations between the state and other public/private persons or the interactions between private citizens.

An international law is defined as a law that governs the conduct of independent nations in their relationships with one another. Most international laws consist of customary international laws which have been established by consistent international practices with consent among nations. However, positive and voluntary agreements are required to conclude codified international laws such as treaties, charters, and protocols.

Chapter 3

The Interpretation and Effectiveness of Law

Section 1. The Interpretation of Law

Ⅰ. Definition

The interpretation of law is defined as the theoretical or technical operation of law in order to systematically understand law, and in order to specify the meaning of the law according to its purpose in the process of application. For example, in the interpretation of Civil Act, the meanings and contents of provisions are understood under the circumstance that considers their objective purposes and social background of the time. It is true that the codified law cannot expect and encompass all the living relations of the time which are diverse and variable. Therefore, to keep flexibility for social development, the codified law cannot help but adopt general and abstract provisions.

Ⅱ. The methods of interpretation

1. The types of interpretation

(1) Grammatical interpretation and logical interpretation

A grammatical interpretation is defined as an interpretation by which a provision is understood exclusively by the words themselves. A provision is interpreted word for word, and thus it is also called linguistic interpretation. A codified law is interpreted first by a grammatical interpretation, and thus the grammatical interpretation is the most fundamental and initiative-stepped type of legal interpretation.

A logical interpretation is defined as an interpreting method through which the objective meaning of law will be sought. Given the provisions of law, the method allows to interpret those provisions depending not only on the literal meaning of words themselves but also on the whole logical structure of the law, taking into account the organic or logical relations of the provisions, the purpose or intent of legislation, and the results of application of the law.

(2) Contrary interpretation and analogical interpretation

A contrary interpretation is defined as the process of interpreting and applying a provision in the circumstance in which, if there occurs an opposite situation to the condition described by the provision, it is assumed that its legal effect is also the opposite to the legally expected one. For example, Article 800 of the Civil Act states that "Any adult person may freely enter into a matrimonial engagement." According to the contrary interpretation, any minor who has not arrived at the marriageable age cannot freely enter into a matrimonial engagement. The contrary interpretation is not always reasonable even though it seems to be logically natural.

An analogy denotes that similarity exists in some characteristics of things that are otherwise not alike. And reasoning by analogy involves referring to a case that concerns unrelated subject matter but is governed by the same general principles and applying those principles to the case at hand. An analogical interpretation, therefore, is defined as the interpreting method in which a similar provision may be used when there is no law or precedent (prior case close in facts and legal principles) in point. Let's look at an example.

In the present Civil Act there are no provisions on unincorporated associations, and provisions on juristic persons are applied analogically. The reason why an analogical interpretation can be acceptable is in the thought that two or more things that are similar to each other in some respects are also similar in other respects.

Ⅲ. The application of law

After the controversy over concrete facts has been settled and the meanings of related legal provisions are clearly determined, the application of law comes next. The application of law proceeds with the method of syllogistic reasoning in which one proposition (the conclusion) is inferred from two others (the premises) of a certain form, i.e. categorical proposition; in the categorical proposition, the abstract legal provisions represent the major premise, while the concrete facts represent the minor premise. This stage of applying law is the most important and essential part in the process of realizing law.

Because legal enforcement produces significant effects on the interests of parties (related people), fairness and accuracy in applying law are always required. Thus, there are many legal and institutional devices in order to achieve fairness and accuracy during the process of juristic and administrative procedures.

Section 2. The Effectiveness of Law

Law is a standard that rules the social life of human beings. Its vital power resides in whether or not it is realized properly in society. Thus, this is the issue of the effectiveness of law, which is concerned with whether or not law can be meaningfully applicable in reality.

Fig.3.1. Methods of law interpretation

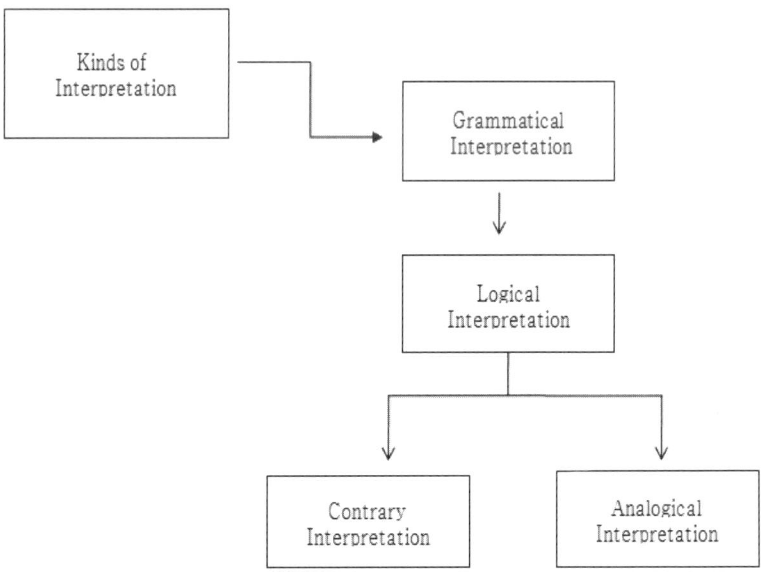

There are two aspects of the effectiveness of law - substantive effectiveness and formal effectiveness. Substantive effectiveness is related to the requirement that any standard should be meaningfully applicable in real society. Formal effectiveness is relevant to the question of how temporally, spatially, and personally effective positive law is under the influences of historical, social, and political factors in the society.

I. The substantive effectiveness of law

1. The validity of law

The fact that a law has effectiveness means it is being meaningfully applied in real society. This normative aspect of legal effectiveness is called validity of law. Validity of law means that the law has authority and regulatory function.

2. The relation between validity and availability of law

To attain its effectiveness, a law must correspond between normative validity and realistic availability. If any of these are lacking, a law loses its value as a positive law. For example, if a law has validity but not availability, it cannot work as a positive law to rule real society. Vice versa, if a law has availability but not validity, it can be nothing but an unjust law.

Philosophers of natural law have regarded any positive law which is against natural law as unjust law. But whether a law is unjust or not should be decided not from individual viewpoints, but from the point of universal legal philosophies of the time. If, based on any individual subjective judgment, a positive law is disregarded or citizens refuse to obey it, before long, our society could be in a state of anarchy.

Ⅱ. The formal effectiveness of law

1. The temporal effectiveness

(1) The temporal effectiveness of law explains where the effectiveness starts and where it finishes. In general, a law carries effectiveness from the enforcement date to the repealed date, and this duration is called a 'period of effectiveness' or an 'effective period'. Customary law (lex non scripta) is effective from the established date, while codified law (lex scripta) is effective from the promulgated date. That is, in the case of codified law, unlike customary law, it needs to be promulgated before its enforcement in order to be legally effective.

Also, a law loses its effectiveness by repeal of the law. The repeal of the law can be divided into two types - expressed repeal with the description of provisons and implied repeal without the description of provisons.

(2) The effectiveness of law is limited by its temporal space. A law is applied only to incidents that occur after the enforcement date, but not to those that occurred before the enforcement date. This is known as the principle of non-retroactivity, meaning that people should be free from retroactive law. However, owing to the reality of society and the pursuit of social justice, there are some exceptions allowed to this principle.

(3) According to the principle of temporal effectiveness, the new law shall be applied when the repeal of old law and the enforcement of new law exist simultaneously. It is the basic principle that the old law shall be applied to the incidents that occurred in the time of old law, ; while the new law shall be applied to the incidents occurring in the time of new law.

2. Personal effectiveness

Personal effectiveness of law explains to whom a law shall be applied. In general, the principle of territorial privilege for jurisdiction (the principle under which sovereign state has jurisdiction over incidents committed within the borders) is applied by priority, and the principle of personal jurisdiction (the principle under which sovereign state has jurisdiction over incidents committed by its people) is applied subsidiarily. However, there are some exceptions allowed. According to the principle of personal jurisdiction, in general, a law shall be applied to all citizens equally. But a special law shall be applied to only a few restricted people, not all citizens. For example, the State Public Officials Act is applied to only public officials and the Labor Standards Act is applied to only employers and employees. According to the principle of territorial privilege for jurisdiction, generally a law should be applied to all the people within the national borders. But, there are some exceptions to this principle too. (These will be discussed in the next section.)

3. Spatial effectiveness

Spatial effectiveness of law explains where a law shall be applied validly. In general, a law is effective within the whole territory of the nation. By the principle of territorial privilege for jurisdiction, the law of The Republic of Korea shall be applied equally to a person who resides in the territory of the nation including territorial lands, waters, and skies, regardless of his (or her) nationality.

However, there are exceptions acceptable to this principle. There is a law that is valid only within the restricted area where the law defines as its territorial range of application. For example, many local governments' regulations of the Local Government Act, and the Town Planning and Zoning Act are valid only within certain areas defined by the laws. Incidents involving warships, merchant ships, and airplanes of a certain country shall be under the jurisdiction of the nation's domestic laws even if those incidents occurred in the high seas or in other countries' territories. It is also possible that any foreign country's laws can substitute for domestic laws because of political reasons. Examples are incidents in occupied territories, mandated territories, and places where a consular jurisdiction is applicable.

Chapter 4 Rights and Duties

Section 1. Juridical Relation

Ⅰ. Definition

A person's living relations are very diverse, though not all of these relations are always regulated by law. Among many personal relations, only some are regulated by law, and we call these juridical relations. Juridical relations are distinguished from other relations (relations that have no legal force) in that these relations are compelled to be fulfilled by law. However, the distinction between juridical relations and other relations is still ambiguous. For example, there is what is called 'goodwill relation', which is generally considered to be a distinguished concept from the juridical relation in that it has no legal force. But lately, as goodwill relations have also come to gain some legal force, it has become very hard to distinguish between goodwill relations and juridical relations nowadays.

Juridical relations, which are basically constituted with rights and duties (obligations), have been developed historically from duty-centric to right-centric. That is, originally they had been status-relationships which imposed only obligations in ancient and medieval times. But they have been changed into right-centric relationships in modern times. Recently, however, these juridical relations are changed again into duty-centric relationships as the social, public, and obligational nature of rights are requested.

Fig.4.1. Legal relation

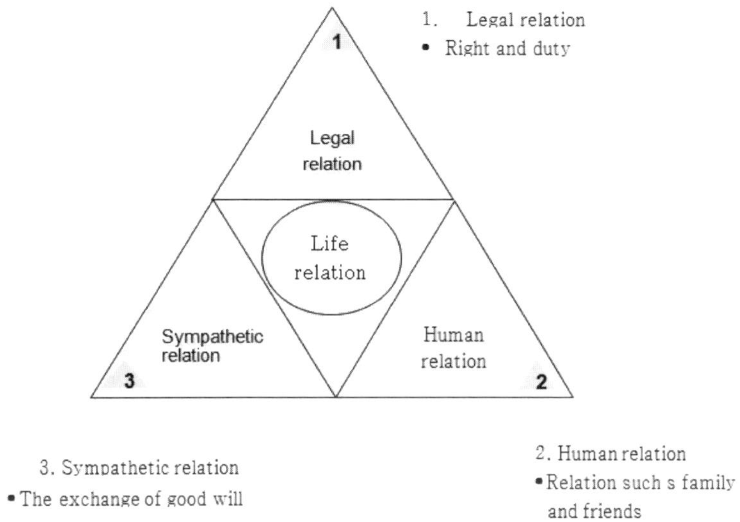

Ⅱ. Rights

1. The nature of rights

It is almost impossible to define the concept of rights straightforwardly. However, to think of the concept of rights as generally as possible, it can be said that a right can be defined as 'legal power allowed for personal interests'. That is, rights are defined as the legal entitlements endowed to a certain person by the law for the purpose of his (or her) enjoyment of certain interests in livelihood.

2. The classification of rights

Rights are classified into two types - public right and private right. The former is allowed by public law such as the Constitution, Criminal Act, etc cetera, while the latter is allowed by private law such as Civil Act, Commercial Act, etc cetera.

According to the attributes, rights are also classified into three representative kinds as follows.

(1) Property rights

Property rights are generally distinguished from other kinds of rights in that they have economic values in their intrinsic attributes. Claims (chose in action), real rights (chose in possession), and intellectual property rights are some examples of property rights.

(2) Personal rights

Personal rights are distinguished from other rights in that they have inherently personal interests which cannot exist apart from the subject of rights. The right to life, personal liberty, the rights of honor, credit, portrait, and privacy are the examples of personal rights.

(3) Family rights

Family rights are distinguished from other rights in that they are related to the status of family intrinsically. Parental rights and the right to claim for support are examples of family rights.

3. Concepts differentiated from rights

(1) Authority

Authority is defined as the justification and right to exercise some juridical acts validly in the area of public and private laws. That is, if power is defined as the ability to influence somebody to do something that he/she would not have normally done, authority refers to the legitimacy (or the justification and right) to exercise that power. The authorities of the President in the Constitution, the authorities of public servants in the administrative laws, and the authorities of directors/agents in the Civil Act are examples of various authorities.

(2) Competence (Competency)

Competence is defined as individual sub-actions derived from a certain right. That is, where there is a right, there are various competences. For example, from the right of ownership of an article, there are various competences - competences to use, to take the profits of, and to dispose of the article owned.

(3) Power

Power is defined as the ability to control over other person or group. In other words, power is a kind of commanding authority, the ability to influence a person or group to do something that he/she/they would not have done otherwise. Unlike violence, power is the legal force to compel other person or group to obey.

(4) Reflective interests

Reflective interests are indirect interests which are gained as by-products from a legal provision. That is to say, people can enjoy the interest from a reflective interest, but cannot claim it as a legal right. Thus, it is not the case of awarding people a concrete legal power positively, but the case of allowing people to enjoy naturally actual (or legal) interests of by-products according to a legal provision.

To distinguish legal rights from reflective interests in the concrete depends wholly on the contents of the legal provisions.

Fig.4.2. Concept of distinguishing rights

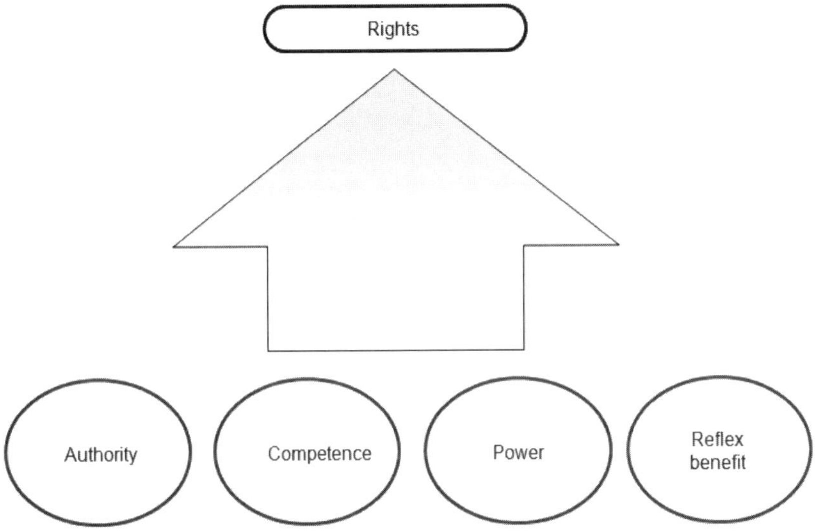

Ⅲ. Obligations (Duties)

1. Definition

An obligation (a duty) in this case is a legal requirement to take some course of action. An obligator must perform his/her obligation regardless of his/her will. Obligations are classified into two types -feasance and non-feasance (forbearance). The former is the obligation to take the indicated action positively, while the latter is the obligation to take the indicated action negatively.

2. The classification of obligations

According to the objectives, obligations (duties) can be divided into two representative types. One is the obligation to the state or to a public institution, such as the obligation to pay taxes, the obligation of national defense, the obligation to receive an education, etc.; the other is the obligation to other states imposed by treaty and other international law.

Ⅲ. Exercise of rights

1. Exercise of rights

(1) Freedom to exercise rights

In principle, it is the freedom of the holder of a right whether or not to exercise that right. But there are exceptions to this principle too. For example, in the case of parental authority, which is granted to help others, the holder has no freedom in whether or not they choose to exercise their right. In that case, the holder of the right has the obligation to exercise that right.

(2) Limitation on the exercise of rights

Clause 1, Article 2 of the Civil Act provides "The exercise of rights and the performance of duties shall be in accordance with the principle of trust and good faith." Also, the second clause of Article 2 describes "No abuse of rights shall be permitted." These are called the 'principle of trust and good faith' and the 'principle of no abuse of rights' respectively.

① The principle of trust and good faith

The principle of trust and good faith states that the exercise of rights and the performance of duties shall be in accordance with the principle of trust and good faith. The principle of trust and good faith may not accept contradictory behavior of one's conduct. However, if the other party had a reasonable and justifiable expectation because the holder of a right had not exercised his/her right for a long time, then it is generally accepted in principle that for the holder to exercise the right again is against the principle of trust and good faith.

② The principle of no abuse of rights

If the exercise of rights is against public and social nature, and therefore is against the principle of trust and good faith, then this exercise of rights shall not be approved as a justifiable exercise. As a result, such exercise of rights cannot be legally valid. This is the principle of no abuse of rights. It is a companion principle to the principle of trust and good faith and also a jurisdictional norm (*Entscheidungsnorm*), a behavioral norm, and a peremptory norm (*jus *cogens*).

For the mechanism of abuse of rights to be applicable, above all, the right itself must exist and that right has to be also exercised positively or negatively. To be relevant to the abuse of rights, at first that abuse must be objectively against the social order and the extent of relevance must be also markedly appropriable to the doctrine of the principle of no abuse of rights. And secondly, from the point of interests, there must exist a noticeable imbalance between the exerciser and the counterpart.

Section 2. The Subject of Rights

Ⅰ. Legal capacity

All persons shall be subjects of rights and duties throughout their lives. Legal capacity is the eligibility to be subjects of rights. And, in relation to the concept of legal capacity of rights, the capacity to be subjects of duties (or obligations) is called the capacity to take responsibilities. As for the scope of legal capacity, the Constitution describes as follows : "All citizens shall be equal before the law, and there shall be no discrimination in political, economic, social or cultural life on account of sex, religion or social status."

Ⅱ. Capacity to act (Capacity for action)

The capacity to act means the eligibility to perform any meaningful juristic act by oneself. The capacity to act is distinguished from the capacity to take on liabilities under the tort law.

1. Incompetent persons

(1) Minor (cf. Majority)

A minor shall obtain the consent of his/her guardian by law to perform any juristic act : *Provided that* exceptions shall be made in cases where the juristic act concerned is one merely to acquire rights or to be relieved from obligations. But even if a minor performed any juristic act without the consent of his/her guardian, the juristic act is none the less not invalid until the minor cancels it. That is, the juristic act without the consent of an guardian is voidable if the minor does not hope for the effect of it. And when a minor cancels a juristic act, it comes to be void from the beginning. Thus, the effect of voidance is retrospective.

(2) Quasi-incompetent

The quasi-incompetent person is a feeble minded person or a spendthrift who may bring poverty to himself or his family. To be approved as a quasi-incompetent, a person should be adjudged to a quasi-incompetent by a court with the application of the person himself, his spouse, any relative within the fourth degree of relationship, guardian or a public prosecutor.

(3) Incompetent

The incompetent is a person in a habitual condition of mental unsoundness who has been adjudged to incompetent by a court with the application of any of the persons mentioned in Article 9 of the Civil Act. The habitual condition of mental unsoundness means that a person is under the state of no mental capacity. However, to be approved as a incompetent, it must be required the habitual condition of mental unsoundness but not necessarily always being under the state of no mental capacity. Juristic acts performed by incompetents are always voidable.

Chapter 5 Constitutional Law

Section 1. The Concept of Constitutional Law

Constitutional law, which is the fundamental law of the nation, ascertains fundamental rights and duties of people. Constitutional law ascertains governing organizations and governing principles to maximize the protection of fundamental rights. There are restrictions on the exercise of fundamental rights for the safety of the nation, the maintenance of social order, and the benefit of the public. However, violations of rights in essence are not allowed in any case.

Section 2. Basic Principles of Constitution

The principles of the Constitution of the Republic of Korea consist of principles of primary objectives which the nation is willing to achieve. The principles are the sovereignty of the people, the doctrine of democratic government (democracy), the doctrine of law-abiding country (constitutionalism), and the doctrine of the social welfare state.

1. Sovereignty of the people

The second clause of Article 1 of the Constitution states that "The sovereignty of the Republic of Korea shall reside in the people, and all state authority shall emanate from the people." Thus, the power and authority to decide national policies originates from the people. Exemplary systems based on the sovereignty of the people are the representational system of national assembly and president, the political party system, the local autonomy, the career civil service system, the separation of powers, and constitutionalism.

Fig.5.1. Principle of Democracy

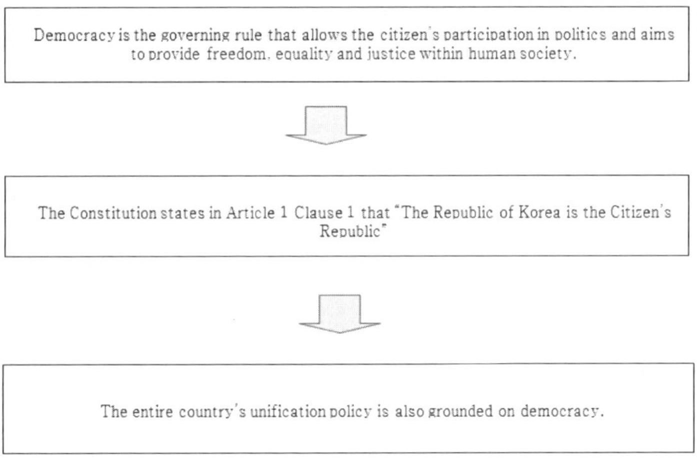

2. The doctrine of democratic government (Democracy)

The preamble of the Constitution states that "by further strengthening the basic free and democratic order", and the first clause of Article 1 states that "The Republic of Korea shall be a democratic republic." Although the democracy is defined in several ways, it is meant as a ruling system of the people to achieve liberty, equality, and justice through the political participation of the people. The constitutional court of Korea defines democracy as a constitutional ruling system based on autonomy, liberty, and equality of the people.

3. The doctrine of the law-abiding country (Constitutionalism)

According to constitutionalism, the rights and freedoms of people can only be restricted within laws established by the national assembly. The second clause of Article 37 of the Constitution states that "The freedoms and rights of citizens may be restricted by Act only when necessary for national security, the maintenance of law and order of public welfare. Even when such a restriction is imposed, no essential aspect of freedom or right shall be violated."

4. The doctrine of social welfare statism

The preamble of the Constitution states that "To destroy all social vices and injustice, and to afford equal opportunities to every person and provide for the fullest development of individual capabilities in all fields, including political, economic, social and cultural life … to elevate the quality of life for all citizens". Also, Article 10 states that "All citizens shall be assured of human dignity and worth and have the right to pursue happiness." Therefore, to build social welfare, the Constitution protects the right to receive an education (Article 31), the right to live a life worthy of human beings (Article 34), the right of workers to receive higher than minimum wage (Article 32), the right of livelihood protection (Article 34), and the right of marriage and family life (Article 36).

Section 3. Fundamental Rights

1. Fundamental rights

Fundamental rights are rights of the people guaranteed by the Constitution. While human rights as natural rights are protected even if there is no government to assure, fundamental rights including rights to live are protected under a government.

2. Rights to pursue happiness and to maintain human dignity

The first clause of Article 10 states that "All citizens shall be assured of human dignity and worth and have the right to pursue happiness." Therefore, the Constitution protects the right to life, the right of name, the right of respect, the right of publicity. The right to pursue happiness is a right to feel contentment without pain as a human being.

3. Rights to equality

The first clause of Article 11 of the Constitution states that "All citizens shall be equal before law, and there shall be no discrimination in political, economic, social or cultural life on account of sex, religion or social status." The equal protection of the laws is divisional equality which allows logical distinction, and it is not average equality that requires everyone to be treated equally.

4. Fundamental rights of freedom

Fundamental rights of freedom protect people from infringement and interference by the government. Thus, the Constitution guarantees personal liberty (Article 12), the freedom of residence and the right to move at will (Article 14), the freedom of occupation (Article 15), residential liberty (Article 16), the right of privacy (Article 17), the right of property (article 23), the freedom of conscience (Article 19), the freedom of religion (Article 20), the freedom of learning and the arts (Article 22), and the freedom of speech and the press, of assembly and association (Article 21).

5. Fundamental rights to live (Social right)

Fundamental rights to live assure that the government provides to a minimum all the necessary conditions to live. Fundamental rights to live are thus distinguished from fundamental rights of freedom which keep the government from interfering in personal life. The Constitution guarantees the right to live a life worthy of human beings (the first clause of Article 34), the right to receive an education (Article 31), the right to work (Article 32), and the right to independent association, collective bargaining and collective action (Article 33).

Fig.5.2. Content of Basic Rights

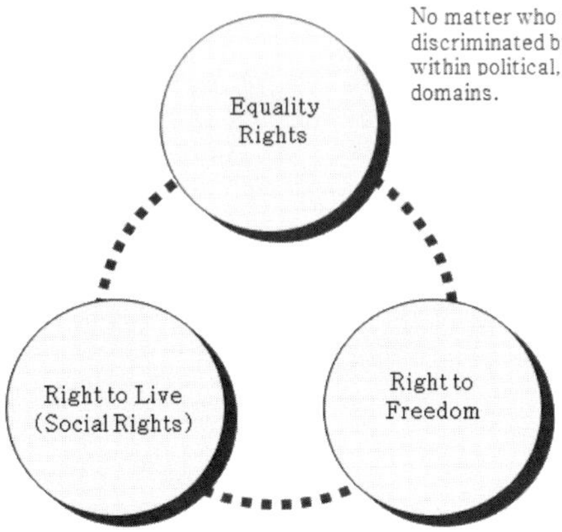

Section 4. Restriction of Fundamental Rights

The second clause of Article 37 of the Constitution states that "The freedoms and rights of citizens may be restricted by Act only when necessary for national security, the maintenance of law and order or for public welfare. Even when such a restriction is imposed, no essential aspect of freedom or right shall be violated." Thus, the scope of restriction and formality should comply with this limitation of the clause. Personal liberty, the freedom of the press, or the right to property can be restricted within laws to ensure national security, to maintain law and order, or to provide public welfare. However, the restrictions on fundamental rights are allowed within the excess of prohibition or the principle of proportionality, which specifies the limits of legitimacy, the appropriateness of means, and balance in the benefit and protection of law. Even when such a restriction is imposed by laws, no law is allowed to violate the essential aspect of the fundamental rights.

Chapter 6

Law of Prohibition on Gender Discrimination

Section 1. Prohibition on Employment Discrimination on The Basis of Gender Identity

1. Definition

An employer shall neither discriminate against workers on the basis of gender, nor take discriminatory treatment in relation to terms and conditions of employment on the ground of nationality, religion, or social status (Article 6 of the Labor Standards Act).

Fig.6.1. Irregular discrimination

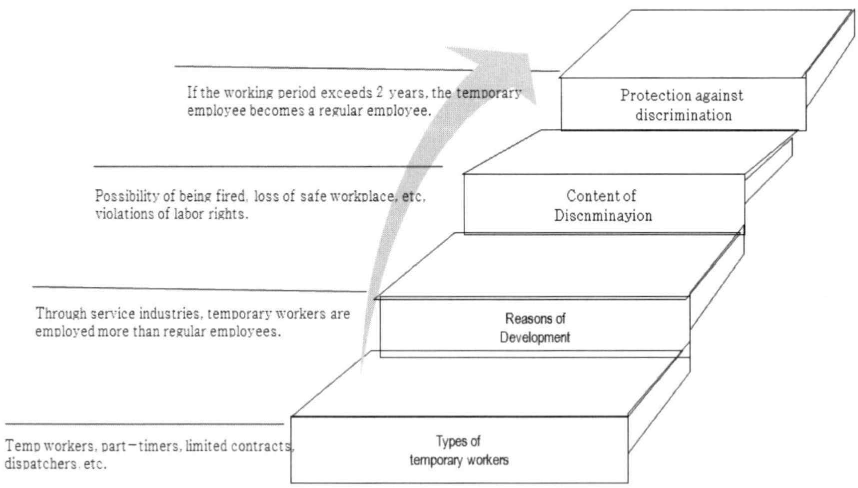

This is the embodiment of the principle of equality before the law, which is stated in the Article 11 of the Constitution, in the relations between employees and employers.

(1) Equality before the law

According to the Article 11 (1) of the Constitution, all citizens shall be equal before the law, and there shall be no discrimination in political, economic, social, or cultural life on account of sex, religion or social status. And the Constitution also provides those equal rights such as an equal opportunity to receive an education, the prohibition on work place discrimination against female workers, gender equality in marriage and family life, and so on.

Discriminative treatment is the practice of treating one person or group of people less fairly or less well than other people or groups without any justifiable reason. Article 6 of the Labor Standards Act describes equal treatment; any kind of discriminative treatment shall not be allowed at the workplace regardless of whether it is before or after employment. That is, Article 6 of the Labor Standards Act is applied to not only affairs before employment but also working conditions after being employed such as working hours, wage, safety, health care, and so on.

2. Prohibition on discriminative treatment between men and women

(1) The standard of judgment about discriminative treatment

① The range of discrimination

Article 2 of the Equal Employment Opportunity and Work Family Balance Assistance Act describes that discriminations include not only direct discriminatory treatment, but also indirect discrimination. For these two concepts, the Act has separate provisions respectively.

The direct discriminatory treatment means that an employer discriminates against a worker in employment or working conditions, or takes any other disadvantageous measures without any justifiable reason, on grounds of gender, marriage, status within family, pregnancy or childbirth, etc. Indirect discrimination are cases in which, even if the employer equally implements equal employment or working conditions for both men and women, the number of one gender capable of satisfying such conditions is remarkably fewer in comparison with the opposite gender, and thus causing disadvantageous results to the opposite gender. (the said conditions may not be attested to be justifiable).

② Non-discriminative treatments

Temporary affirmative actions: such cases in which a specific gender is inevitably requested owing to the characteristics of duties; cases where measures are taken for protecting motherhood, such as pregnancy, childbirth and lactation of female workers; and the cases of positive employment improvement measures, where measures to favorably treat one specific gender in order to eliminate existing employment discrimination between men and women, are regarded as neither direct discriminatory treatments nor indirect discriminations.

(2) Equal pay for work of equal value

① Definition

Among various working conditions, the most important is the factor of wage. Here, the concept of wage includes not only the wage itself, but also discriminatory treatments on the wage structure, the wage payment plan, and the payment method, etc. However, an employer can distinguish or discriminate between male and female workers according to job specifications, performance of duties, efficiency of job performance, and skills, etc. And these discriminative treatments are not against the principle of equal pay for work of equal value.

② The standards for work of equal value

The employer shall provide equal pay for work of equal value within an identical business. The work of equal value is defined as the same or similar work between men and women from the point of skills, labor, responsibility, working conditions, etc. In spite of the essential difference between two comparative works, if the value of work is estimated similar by job evaluation, they are also regarded as works for equal value. (The Article 8 of the Equal Employment Opportunity and Work Family Balance Assistance Act)

(3) Discrimination on retirement age

If an employer establishes the lower age limit for female workers than that of male workers, it may be considered to be gender discrimination. Therefore, if an employer establishes different age limit between men and women such as 58 for male workers and 50 for female workers respectively and, at the same time, if there were no justifiable distinction-standards (i.e. the standards of requested genders according to characteristics of duties, concrete job classifications, etc.) in the collective agreement or in the employment regulation, the employer's discriminative establishment of age limit belongs to the gender discrimination.

(4) Marriage-grounded retirement system

① It shall not be permitted as a discriminative treatment to dismiss a female employee only because of her marriage unless the job has any justifiable reason for a married woman unable to undertake in light of the characteristic of the work. ②After an employee was recruited, although an employer originally recruited a female worker under the condition that she should be unmarried, it is against the law as a gender discrimination if the employer dismissed her because of her marriage. ③Related with the marriage-grounded retirement system, both the female employees' retirement for childbirth and the female-employee-preferred workforce reduction are also examined similarly as the logic of marriage-grounded retirement system.

Section 2. Sexual Harassment

1. The definition of sexual harassment

Sexual harassment is interpreted as the behaviors of unwelcome sexual temptation, unwelcome requests for sexual favors, and other verbal or physical conduct of a sexual nature. According to the view of the U.S. Supreme Court, sexual harassment is a range of behaviors in which a superior wrongly abuses their authority towards the inferior in order to request unwelcome sexual favors. In Korea, sexual harassment is defined as the unwelcome requests for sexual favors, which is distinguished from sexual violence, sexual molestation, and stalking in the criminal law.

2. The types of sexual harassment

(1) Physical behavior

In this category, there are physical contacts like kissing, hugging, embracing at the back, etc.; physical touches on the special part of the body like the breast, the hip, etc.; the coercion of the other into massaging or caressing; and so on.

(2) Verbal behavior

Here the most typical example is the telling (or calling, writing, e-mailing) of filthy or obscene jokes. Other behaviors such as a sexual comparison or evaluation of the outward appearance, an intentional asking or disseminating the other's sexual privacy, a conciliation or coercion of sexual favors, etc. also belong to the category of this verbal behavior.

(3) Visual behavior

This includes behaviors such as putting up or showing obscene photographs, pictures, or publications, and posting them in the cyber bulletin board, and also exposing or fondling his/her specific part of the body in relation to the sexuality, etc.

3. Types of behavior unable to be recognized as sexual harassment

Behaviors such as the sexual relationship under love or friendship, family violence affairs which are under judicial request for remedy, affairs which occur away from employment sites like offices, public institutions, schools, etc., rough-talking, running of errands, and so on cannot belong to the scope of sexual harassment, even though they may belong to the ill-mannered behaviors. Also, 1 year after a sexual harassment incident occurs, it is no longer considered valid as sexual harassment.

Fig.6.2. Actions not considered to be sexual harassment

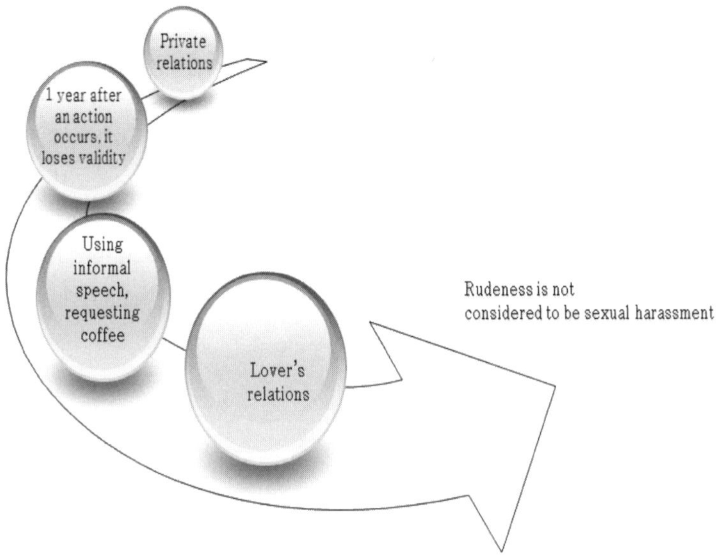

4. The establishment and remedy for sexual harassment

(1) Standard of what is considered sexual harassment

It is unreasonable to apply one objective standard of judgment to all affairs uniformly because the concept of sexual harassment itself is very abstract. For example, say that 2 people, person A and person B, both receive the same treatment. Person A may perceive that treatment as sexual harassment, while person B may not feel affected at all by the incident.

Therefore, whether sexual harassment has occurred or not needs to be judged from the viewpoint of a general citizen. That is, a reasonable person should be the judge of an incident of sexual harassment. For example, if an employee received unfair treatment in the workplace (dismissal, discrimination in assignment to a department, failure to be promoted, etc.) on account of their disregard of the employer's sexual demands, or, if any unwelcomed sexual favors occurred by an employer utilizing their position within a workplace and the victim felt humiliated or disgusted, it can be said that sexual harassments exist in spite of the place they happened.

(2) The remedy for sexual harassment

To remedy sexual harassment, first of all, the acceptance of applications about sexual harassments has to be proceeded. Counselling and investigation processes must be followed. (It is better to use hearing from the witness than to use confrontation with the suspect for protection of privacy.) Once sexual harassment has been identified, appropriate measures should be taken, such as the transference of the sexual offender, warning, placement on a waiting list, suspension from office, dismissal, etc.

Chapter 7 Crime and Criminal Law

Section 1. Crime

Ⅰ. Crime and punishment (Criminal law)

A criminal law relates criminal conducts with resultant punishments. That is, a criminal law regulates what crimes and how criminals are punished. For example, Article 250 of the Criminal Act states that "A person who kills another shall be punished by death, or imprisonment for life or at least 5 years." The conduct of "one killing another" constitutes crime of murder, and the resultant punishment of "by death, or imprisonment for life or at least 5 years" shall be sentenced.

Ⅱ. The principle of legality

Crimes and resultant punishments are defined in criminal law. The principle of legality means that criminality and punishability of an act shall be determined by law. Only criminal law defines what behavior society regards as wrongful. Also, criminal law defines the type and extent of punishments. If there is no law which defines as a crime for a specific act, then there is no punishment at all regardless of wrongness.

Ⅲ. Criminal Act

By the principle of legality, criminal law defines crimes. For example, "murder" is defined by law as a crime for killing another person, and "larceny" is for stealing property of other people. Each provision of criminal law defines all elements to be convicted for the specific crime.

1. Elements for criminality

There are three elements required to be convicted of a crime: configuration requirement, illegality, and liability. To be convicted as a criminal act, an act must meet the configuration requirements for a specific crime, be illegal, and be performed by a liable person.

(1) Configuration requirement

Configuration requirement is the first element to be considered for criminal act to be convicted.

① Causality

For certain crimes, criminal act must have a result followed by the action which constitutes a specific crime. For example, killing a victim inevitably results in death in the case of murder. There must be cause and effect for criminal act to be convicted.

② Intention and negligence

Intention is the state of mind to commit criminal act, composed of both recognition and willingness. Recognition is the act of recognizing or identifying someone or something, and willingness is the attempt, desire, or volition to do or express something. In case of taking another person's cat by mistake, it is not larceny due to the lack of intention.

Negligence, which means lack of reasonal care, is an act performed through the ignorance of the fact that composes constituents of crime. There are two types of negligence: negligence with recognition and negligence without recognition. Negligence with recognition occurs under the recognition of constituents of crime, and negligence without recognition does without any recognition.

(2) Illegality

Illegality is defined as an act that violates a law, yet is established as socially acceptable. If an act satisfies configuration requirements of specific crimes, it is assumed that it is illegal, except in special cases. The special cases that are not convicted are justifiable acts, self-defense, and necessity.

① Justifiable act

Justifiable acts, which are not punishable, are acts conducted in accordance with law or in pursuance of accepted business practices. Examples of acts conducted in accordance with law are performances of public officers on duty, corporal punishments by teachers, labor disputes of unions, and medical practices of doctors.

② Self-defense

An act which is performed in order to prevent impending and unjust infringement of one's own or another person's legal interest shall not be punishable if there are reasonable grounds for that act. For example, self-defense against the unexpected usage of deadly weapons in ordinary fisticuffs shall not be punishable. However, when a preventive act has exceeded normal limits, the punishment maybe mitigated or remitted according to the extenuating circumstances.

③ Necessity

An act which is performed in order to avoid impending danger against the one's own or another person's legal interest shall not be punishable if there are reasonable grounds for that act. An excessive act to a certain degree is allowed to escape from imminent dangers including natural phenomena and animal attacks. For example, intrusion into another person's house to avoid armed robbery shall not be punishable under the name of necessity. Exceeding speed limits on the road to escort critical patients in an emergency shall not be punishable for the violation of traffic law.

(3) Liability

Liability is a matter of blamableness for a criminal act. A criminal act is blamable when the offender acts against the law instead of following it. Under certain circumstances, an offensive conduct is blameless or less blamable, and it is a matter of liable capacity.

① Liable capacity

A liable capacity is a capacity to act legally, and a capacity to receive blame for illegal acts. Whether there is a liable capacity or not determines whether the criminal act is punishable or not. A person with lack of liable capacity has no ability to distinguish bad from good or no ability to exercise his/her own will. For example, insanity defense is allowed since legal conduct is not expected of a mentally ill person.

② Criminal minors and incompetents

The act of a person under fourteen years of age shall not be punished. Also, the act of a person who is unable to make discriminations or to control one's will because of a mental disorder shall not be punished. For the conduct of a person who is deficient in the above mentioned abilities because of mental disorder, the punishment shall be mitigated.

Section 2. Penalty

Criminal law defines constituent elements and resultant penalty for each crime to proclaim social virtues to be protected and prohibited conducts to be punishable.

1. Crimes against legal interests of private citizens

Crimes against legal interests of private citizens are crimes defined to protect life, body, freedom, honor, credit, and private life of a citizen. In liberal democratic society, which esteems human dignity and worth, legal interests of private citizens are the most important interests protected by criminal law, since both the society and the nation exist by the people and for the people.

Fig.7.1. Individual crime and the benefit and protection of the law

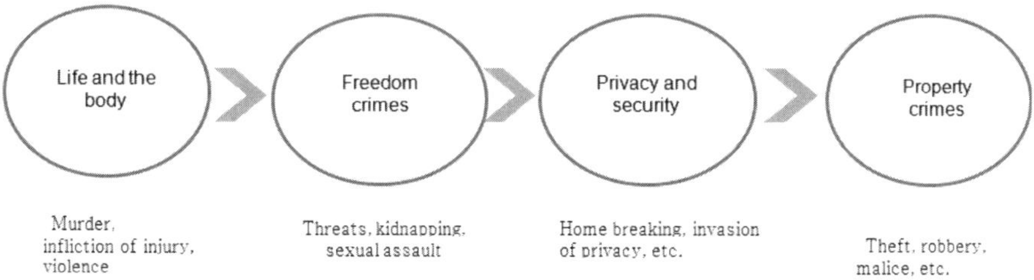

Among crimes against legal interests of private citizens, crimes concerning the life and body of a citizen are crimes which endanger one's life or injure one's body. Examples are crimes of homicide, crimes of inflicting bodily injury and violence, crimes of false arrest and illegal confinement, crimes of kidnapping, and crimes concerning rape and infamous conduct.

2. Crimes against legal interests of society

Crimes against legal interests of society are crimes defined to protect general interests of social life, which constitutes the elementary cohabitation of human beings. Crimes against legal interests of society are different from crimes against legal interests of private citizens in the sense that these are designed not for the individual, but for the whole society. Also, crimes against legal interests of society are different from crimes against legal interests of the nation in the sense that these are designed not for the security of the nation, but for the society. Examples are crimes injurious to public peace, crimes concerning public credibility, crimes concerning public health, crimes of arson and fire caused by negligence, and crimes of traffic obstruction.

Fig.7.2. Social crime and the benefit and protection of the law

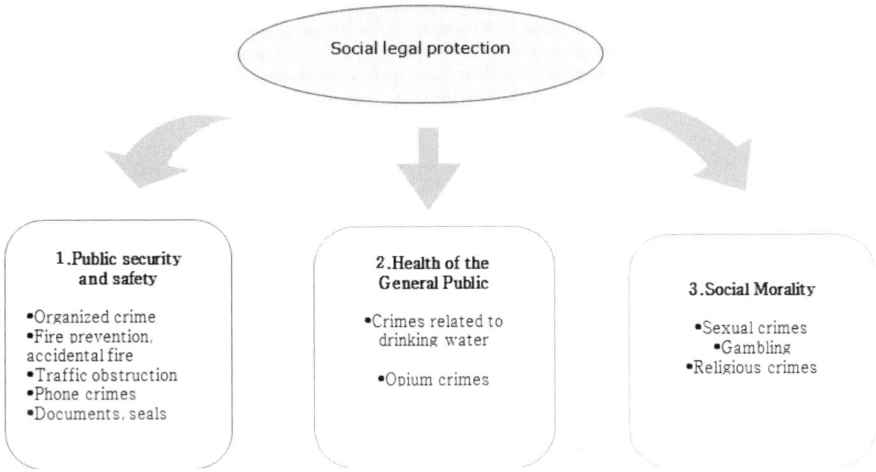

3. Crimes against legal interests of the nation

Crimes against legal interests of the nation are crimes defined to protect security, dignity and function of the nation, and therefore divided into two groups: crimes concerning national security and dignity, and crimes concerning national function. Among crimes concerning national security and dignity, crimes concerning insurrection and foreign aggression are crimes against national security. On the other hand, crimes concerning the national flag are crimes against national dignity. Examples of crimes concerning national function are crimes concerning the duties of public officials and obstruction of the performance of official duties, crimes of escape and harboring criminals, crimes of perjury and destruction of evidence, and crimes of false accusation.

Chapter 8 Administrative Law

Section 1. Law of Administrative Action

1. Concept of administrative law

Administrative law includes laws concerning administrative organizations, administrative actions, and remedies against administration. Administrative law provides the legal foundation of administrative agencies, including the nation and public entities. Also, the law gives authority of administrative actions and clarifies relations between administrative agencies. Administrative law describes legal relation between private citizens and administrative agencies, and provides remedy against administrative actions.

2. Characteristics of administrative law

Characteristics of administrative law are the characteristics of laws concerning administrative actions, and these characteristics are the power of officiation, the power of definiteness, and the power of enforcement. All of them are awarded for public interests.

(1) Power of officiation

Power of officiation is the presumption of legitimacy for administrative actions. This power of officiation affects all parties of administration including interested persons, other administrative agencies, and other countries.

(2) Power of definiteness

Power of definiteness means that all administrative actions shall not be canceled even if there are flaws. Power of definiteness consists of power of no dispute and power of no change. Power of no dispute means that any dispute is not allowed after the expiration of the appealable period or after the conclusion of litigation, even if an administrative action is defective. Power of no change means that an administrative agency in charge shall not change any administrative action for cancelation or alteration.

(3) Power of enforcement

Self enforcement of administrative law means that the administrative agency shall directly enforce one to perform one's duty in case of nonfulfillment. Execution by The Administrative Agency Act provides legal grounds for general power of enforcement, and the National Tax Collection Act does for duty of cash payment in public law. Administrative penalties shall be imposed in the case of non observance.

3. Protection of personal information

(1) Law for the protection of personal information

Article 17 of Constitution states that "The privacy of no citizen shall be infringed" in order to protect personal information. Also, Article 18 states that "The privacy of the correspondence of no citizen shall be infringed" in order to protect all kinds of communication. There are laws such as the Personal Information Protection of Public Institutes Act and the Information and Communication Promotion and Information Protection Act established in order to protect personal information. Personal Information Protection of Public Institutes Act is designed to prevent the improper usage and disclosure of personal information by administrative agencies, and Information and Communication Promotion and Information Protection Act is designed to prevent service providers from collecting, maintaining, using, and furnishing personal information improperly.

(2) Protectable substance of personal information

Personal Information Protection of Public Institute Act is designed to protect personal information that is stored and processed in computers owned by public institutes. Personal information is defined as all original information generated during one's life time, including name and resident registration number.

(3) Restriction on collecting personal information

Personal Information Protection of Public Institutes Act protects personal information processed by computers, including the improper input, storage, modification, searching, and deletion of information. Public institutes cannot collect any personal information which reveals one's belief and ideology in order to protect the fundamental rights of citizen.

(4) Request to read and amend by information provider

An information provider may request in writing to read his/her filed information from the holding public institute. The holding public institute then allows the information provider to read their information within 30 days except in restricted cases. Also, the information provider may request in writing to correct his/her filed information from the holding public institute. In this case, the holding public institute must immediately perform necessary action after research if there is no other law to be applied.

(5) Penalty

A person who changes or erases any personal information with the purpose of interrupting official process of personal information shall be punished by imprisonment for not more than 10 years. A person who reveals, processes without authority, provides to another for use, or improperly uses personal information shall be punished by imprisonment for not more than 3 years or a fine of not more than ten million won.

Section 2. Remedies Against Administrative Problems

1. Administrative damages

Administrative damages are accorded when an administrative act causes any loss to a citizen. The state or nation is responsible for administrative damages, and administrative damages are called national damages. In general, administrative damages consist of negligent liability (tort liability of public officials) and liability for public works.

(1) Tort liability of public officials

Tort liability of public officials is liability caused by illegal acts of public officials with negligence. Tort liability of public officials is applied ① when any loss occurs in the process of public duty, ② when the administrative act is illegally performed intentionally or negligently, and ③ when the loss is caused by an illegal act of a public official.

(2) Damages caused by defects of public works

The nation is liable for any damages caused by defects of public works, since establishment and maintenance of public works are administrative acts. Although Article 758 of Civil Act regulates liability of the possessor or owner of a structure or construction, it is not clear that this article applies to damages caused by defects of public works.

National Damages Act is applicable for damages ① which are caused by public works, ② which are caused by defects in establishment or maintenance, and ③ which result in any loss for a citizen.

2. Administrative indemnity

Administrative indemnity is the system that compensates for the property loss of a person owing to a legal administrative act. Administrative indemnity is designed to protect personal property and to share burden equally. Therefore, through administrative indemnity, all people equally share burden in order to compensate for the loss caused by expropriating or using personal property, or by restriction on personal property right for public interests.

3. Appeal for administration

Appeal for administration is an appeal for any illegal or unfair administrative act performed by an administrative agency. Appeal for administration is not a judicial appeal in the sense that it is concluded by Administrative Appeal Board, which is established in superior authority of the relevant administrative agency. Appeal for administration is a system to remedy personal rights according to the Constitution, since Clause 3 of Article 107 in Constitution states that "Administrative appeals may be conducted as a procedure prior to a judicial trial. The procedure of administrative appeals shall be determined by Act and shall be in conformity with the principles of judicial procedures." Administrative Appeal Act governs procedures of administrative appeals, and other laws also have rules regarding administrative appeals such as petition of objection, application for scrutiny, application for appeal, and request for retrial.

4. Litigation against administration

Litigation against administration is a administrative litigation of judicial court to resolve any dispute over an administrative act. Among litigations against administration, typical litigation is litigation for revocation, which calls for revocation of administrative order. Litigation for revocation is a litigation against any illegal act or adjudication of an administrative agency to claim revocation or alteration which results in discharge of administrative act retroactively.

(1) Procedure of administrative litigation

① Procedure

Prerequisite conditions for administrative litigation are the existence of plaintiff and defendant, and feasance or nonfeasance of administrative agency, which is the substance of dispute calling for revocation or alteration. A revocation litigation may be instituted without an administrative appeal in advance, even if the administrative appeal may be instituted against a disposition in question pursuant to the provisions of Acts and subordinate statutes. Conformable jurisdiction is required, and the period for bringing litigation must not have lapsed to initiate administrative litigation.

② Trial

Court trial begins after the filing of a lawsuit. Trial of administrative litigation is a procedure to distinguish between factual and legal relations and to lead to judgement. At trial of administrative litigation, oral defences are only allowed in principle.

③ Adjudication

Adjudication by court concludes a legal dispute after litigious procedures. There are overruling, dismissal, citation, and citation of part in adjudication.

Chapter 9 Employment Relations

Section 1. The Labor Standards Act

1. Purpose of the Labor Standards Act

According to Article 32 of the Constitution, the standards for working conditions shall be determined the Labor Standards Act in ways so as to guarantee human dignity. This is the main goal of the Labor Standards Act. Accordingly, the purpose of the Labor Standards Act is to set the standards for the conditions of Employment in accordance with the Korean Constitution, thereby securing and improving the living standards of workers and developing a well-balanced economy.

2. Characteristics of the Labor Standards Act

The Labor Standards Act does not only stipulate regulations on public law that deal with labor management and opinion, but also specifies regulations on private law that requires compensation for damages resulting from an employer's violation of the Labor Standards Act, with causes the worker to terminate his/her labor contract.

3. Basic Principles of the Labor Standards Act

(1) Prohibition of lowering working conditions

The conditions of employment provided herein cannot be lowered, thus the parties of employment shall not depress working conditions under the pretext of complying with the Labor Standards Act.

(2) Labor and management's equal decision power

The conditions of employment shall be determined through a mutual agreement between employers and their workers on an equal footing.

(3) Thorough fulfillment of working conditions

Both employers and workers shall comply with the Collective Agreement, the Rules of Employment, and the terms of the labor contract, and both parties shall be obliged to do so in good faith.

(4) Equal treatment

An employer shall not discriminate against any worker on the basis of gender, nor display discriminatory treatment in the conditions of employment on account of nationality, religion or social status.

A) Major example of unequal treatment

① Unequal pay for equal work; The principle of equal treatment is not violated in cases where unequal treatment is effected by work, efficiency, technology, etc. and where it is accounted for by different working conditions, job type, or job characteristics. ② Discrimination due to retirement age; Discrimination against any male or female, due to their reaching retirement age, violates Article 5 of the Labor Standards Act. ③ Retirement on account of marriage; The employer is not allowed to discriminate against any female worker due to her marital status.

B) Examples of unequal treatment on account of nationality, religion and social status.

① Nationality; The purpose of preventing unequal treatment on account of nationality is to protect dual nationality holders and foreign nationals from possible discrimination. ② Religion; It is considered a violation of the law if an employee is actively discriminated on account of his/her religious beliefs or passively discriminated on account of his/her lack of religious affiliation. With the exception of purpose-based companies, it is not deemed a violation if the employee is dismissed due to any behavior that disagrees with the religious or political purpose of his/her company. ③ Social status; The employer shall prohibit unequal treatment or unfair working conditions on account of social class or privileged status.

(5) Prohibition of forced labor

An employer shall not force a worker to work against his own free will through the use of violence, threats, confinement or by any other means that unjustly restrict mental or physical freedom.

(6) Prohibition of violence

Accident or any other mishaps caused by the worker shall not be a legitimate reason for physical or verbal abuse.

(7) Elimination of intermediary exploitation

No one shall intervene in the employment of another person for the purpose of making a profit, nor shall anyone gain benefit as an intermediary unless otherwise provided by law.

(8) Guarantee of exercising civil rights

An employer shall not reject a request from a worker to grant the time necessary to exercise his/her right to suffrage or other civil rights, or to perform official duties during his working hours; however, the time requested may be changed, unless such alteration impedes the exercise of those rights or the performance of those civil duties.

Section 2. Wages

1. Wage Requisites and Judgment Standards

(1) Concept of wage

Article 18 of the Labor Standards Act(Definition of Wages). The term "wages" means wages, salary and any other kind of money or valuables, regardless of its title, which the employer pays to a worker as remuneration for work.

(2) Wage requisites

① Paid by the employer
Given that wages are what the employer pays to employee, the service charge that a worker receives from customers in a hotel or restaurant cannot be considered as wages in principle.

② Remuneration for work
If wages are paid as remuneration for work, cannot be deemed to be wages if the employer renders payment under friendly and favorable terms outside of work, or if the employer provides pay as part of welfare, or if the employee receives reimbursement for actual expenses.

③ Any payment regardless of label

Wages are paid in forms of salary or allowance in general. They are considered wages regardless of under what label the payment is given, if the employer is paying as remuneration for work to the subordinate employee. Accordingly, we shall not estimate information allowance and welfare fee as wages just by their titles, because wages are differentiated by payment conditions.

(3) Concrete criteria of wages

① Money paid under friendly and favorable terms is not considered to be wages.

It is not considered to be wages if paid for optional, courteous, and friendly reasons including congratulatory and consolation allowance, award for QC activities, or money paid favorably to celebrate special occasions such as the Company's foundation days.

② Money paid for actual expenses is not considered to be wages.

Money paid to reimburse actual expenses for the purchase of production instrument such as security equipment is not wages. Reimbursements for purchase of work uniforms, tools and materials, business trip expenses, travelling expenses, account expenses, confidential expenses, and information fees are also not considered to be wages.

③ Welfare fees are not considered to be wages.

The welfare fee in its true meaning is not a wage because it cannot be treated as remuneration for work. However, if paid regularly to all workers in accordance with the Collective Agreement, Rules of Employment or a repeated precedent, it is considered to be wages under the Labor Standards Act.

Section 3. Disciplinary Dismissal

This is a disciplinary action to sever all labor relations with the employee whose violation is so severe that the company cannot expect managerial order without excluding them.

1. Justification Cases for Disciplinary Causes

(1) Negligence of duty

Negligence in the Rules of Employment refer to poor work performance or insincere attendance, and job negligence in behavior displayed partly or entirely by the employees in providing labor service. Therefore, they may be subject to a wage reduction or personnel evaluation, but they are not liable for disciplinary punishment.

Nevertheless, negligence of duty can induce disciplinary punishment in such case where the employee is negligent without permission, or the employee's behavior disrupts order regardless of reporting the cause in advance, or where the employee repeats same mistakes by neglecting warnings from the company.

(2) Work attitude and poor performance

Poor work attitude indicates behavior that degrades work efficiency or reduces productivity due to lack of concentration on duty. Absences without permission, work negligence or frequent tardies can account for evaluating work attitude. Repeated poor work attitude cannot naturally be subject for disciplinary action, but when the employee neglects or does not abide by warnings given by the company, he/she may be subject to disciplinary action.

(3) Company discipline or disorder of rules

Unyielding to company discipline signifies that the employee is disturbing the company's order, violating working rules with unacceptable behavior, violating dress code, etc., which are matters concerning the freedom of private life. Disruption of company order disorganizes team work in the company, thereby disturbing peace and order through behavior that brings negative influences to the company.

In general, company order is regulated in the Rules of Employment. Even if there is no specified regulation concerning it in the Rules of Employment, the employee shall have an additional duty bound by the labor contract, which is not to disturb the company's group activities.

(4) Violation of directions

Refusing to follow directions at work means the employee is neglecting company principles and causing industrial accidents by resisting necessary directions, disobeying them without legitimate reasons, or independently performing a duty that actually requires a superior's permission.

(5) Violation of secret preservation

The employee has an additional duty from the labor contract that obliges them to disclose company secrets to a third party or abuse them.

(6) Prohibition of double employment

Most rules of employment prohibit double employment. The employee shall obtain company's permission prior to becoming a director or employee at a different company or organization, and shall not be employed at an identical or similar type of company for a certain period of time after resigning from the company.

(7) Use of company's facilities without permission

A company's right of facility management is a right to use materials originating from ownership. Namely, an employer as an owner of the property has a right to manage for his/her own purposes. If an employee uses the company's facilities without permission, breaks their functions or interferes with their operations, he/she may be liable for disciplinary punishment for violating the right of facility management.

(8) Interference of business

It is recognized as an interference of duty when an employee interferes with the employer's business without a justifiable reason, obstructs other employee's execution of duty, distorts information, or obstructs operation. One may be sentenced up to five years of imprisonment or be fined up to 15 million won under Article 314 of the Criminal Act.

(9) Delinquencies outside of business and criminal offenses

When an employee's delinquency outside of business affects mutual reliability or human relations with other co-workers inside the company, and disrupts labor relations, it can induce disciplinary punishment. However, such corrupt behavior and immoral conduct pertain to the employee's private life, and may account for social blame, but cannot be the sole cause of disciplinary action in principle. It can only be considered as disciplinary punishment when the offense infringes company order.

(10) Embezzlement, misappropriation and bribes

An employee's embezzlement or misappropriation of company funds is detrimental to the company. Accordingly, the employee is subject to disciplinary punishment if they are in a position requiring financial trust and commits related crimes or misappropriates company property by taking advantage of a proxy right on the business, regardless of the amount considered.

If bribes degrade the company's reputation and dignity of the workers, and harm the company's honor and trustworthiness, then disciplinary action may be taken.

(11) Theft or running away with company possessions

Theft of company property is an insidious behavior of an anti-social nature and is cause for heavy disciplinary punishment. Running away with company possessions without permission also accounts for disciplinary action as a punishment for damaging the company.

(12) Defamation of character

When an employer's reputation is slandered on account of an employee's immoral or illegal conduct, in addition to warning the employee, the employer can also take disciplinary actions.

(13) Misrepresentation of career and falsifying information in the re-

sume

Misrepresentation of career is deemed a justifiable reason for disciplinary punishment, not when it may distort the company's assessment of the employee's labor ability, character, trust, etc, but when it disturbs the structure of working conditions such as wage level and position decision due to past critical misrepresentation of career, or when the falsified information infringes the company's actual order and proves damaging to the employer.

Common examples include misrepresentation of educational achievement and jobs done, concealment of ideology or faith, concealment of imprisonment or disciplinary action data, concealment of full-time labor union's key officials, etc.

Chapter 10 Labor Union

Section 1. Labor Union

Article 33 of the Constitution stipulates the three basic rights of labor are "to enhance working conditions, workers shall have the right to independent association, collective bargaining and collective action". Actions performing the right to independent association are accomplished through a labor union. Labor unions can make a collective bargaining agreement through collective negotiation as an equal counterpart of the employer for the purpose of maintaining and improving the working conditions of the employees to enhance their economic and social status. The labor union can also stage a strike where the employees collectively refuse to work as a means to meet their ends.

1. Requirements to Protect the Labor Union

The labor union shall be established under the substantial requirements of Article 2, subparagraph 4, of the Labor Union and Labor Relations Adjustment Act (hereafter known as the "Labor Union Act") and formal requirements of Article 10 of the Act, so it can be recognized and protected under the general rights of the Labor Union Act.

(1) Positive requirements

The labor union shall be an organization or associated organizations of workers, formed in a voluntary and collective manner upon the workers' initiative for the purpose of maintaining and improving their working conditions and enhancing their economic and social status. These positive requirements must be established by the labor union.

① Subject of rights

The labor union shall be formed under a united organization of workers for the subject of rights.

② Independence

The labor union shall be formed as a collective group by the basic principle of establishment. The labor union represents a group against the employer and shall behave voluntarily and collectively upon the workers' free will without the intervention of the labor office or the employer, otherwise it loses its independence.

③ Purpose

The labor union shall be an organization established for the purpose of maintaining and improving their working conditions and enhancing their economic and social status.

(2) Negative requirements

The labor union shall be free of the following, "negative requirements":

① "In cases where the employer or other persons who always act in the interest of the employer are allowed to join"

This is designed to prevent the labor union from becoming a company union and to promote equality and independence by excluding the employer and other persons who act in the interest of the employer.

② "In cases where most of its expenditures are supported by the employer"

The labor union shall not receive regular subsidies or assistance from the employer, other than the least possible support such as the office, office fixtures, etc.

③ "In cases where its activities are only aimed at mutual support, self improvement and other welfare undertakings"

The labor union shall be designed to improve the working conditions, and so if the labor union exists only for the betterment of welfare, it shall not be recognized as a labor union.

④ In cases where those who are not workers are allowed to join

Provided that a dismissed person who has applied to the Labor

Relations Commission for remedies person who has practices shall not be regarded as a person who is not a worker until a review decision has been made by the Central Labor Relations Commission.

⑤ In cases where its aims are mainly directed at political movements.

The previous Article 12 of the pre-revised Labor Union Act concerning the prohibition of the union's political activities has been deleted, and this new article has been replaced to protect the labor union from losing its purpose.

(3) Formal requirement

Any person who intends to establish a labor union shall submit a report specifying concerned matters, together with the bylaws to the Minister of Labor. Upon receiving the certificate of report, the union shall be recognized as soon as it notifies the Minister of Labor of its establishment.

Section 2. Collective Bargaining and Collective Agreement

1. Concept of collective bargaining

Collective bargaining refers to the negotiation of working conditions by the labor-management council. The labor union and the employer (or employee's association) come to agree collectively on working conditions or other fair rules of labor relations and conclude the Collective Agreement.

2. Collective Bargaining's Party and Person-in-charge

(1) Collective bargaining's party

The collective bargaining's party has the right and duty for collective bargaining and implements it independently.

① Employee side

The bargaining party for the employee shall be a legitimate labor union established under requirements demanded by the Labor Union Act. Thus, temporary strike groups, dismissed employees' groups, company organization, individual employees, or anti-union key members do not have legal authority to demand collective bargaining. Hence, if the employer rejects collective bargaining, it is not recognized as an unfair practice.

In the case where the labor union is formed as an industrial or occupational union, but its union branch or union unit for the individual company is established under proper requirements such as the union bylaws, union officers, etc. in order to act independently, such a union can be a party of collective bargaining for specific contents according to the demands of the union described by the union bylaws or union's resolutions as the party to have the right and duty for negotiation.

② Employer side

The bargaining party for the employer shall be the corporation for the corporate entity or the company owner for a private company. The employers' association has the right to adjust or control its members concerning labor relations.

(2) Person-in-charge of collective bargaining

① Employee side

The representative of a labor union or delegates of a labor union shall have the authority to bargain as person-in-charge of the collective bargaining.

② Employer side

The employer or representative of the employers' association shall be the person- in-charge of the collective bargaining. Here, the employer refers to the company owner in the case of a private company, or the representative director in the case of a corporation. The general manager of the branch office or the chief of the labor affairs department can also be the person-in-charge of the collective bargaining through proxy authority of limited scope or special delegation.

Section 3. Industrial Actions

1. Industrial Disputes

The term "industrial disputes" refers to any controversy or difference arising from disagreements between a labor union and an employer or employers' association concerning the conditions of employment such as wages, working hours, welfare, dismissal, and other issues (Article 2, subparagraph 5, of Labor Union Act).

(1) Disputes arising from disagreements

Disagreements between the two parties are not always considered as industrial disputes. However, if the two parties attempt collective bargaining, but fail to reach an agreement, then their conflict is considered an industrial dispute.

(2) State of disputes

Industrial disputes signify a state of disputes. Accordingly, it is a different concept from an industrial action under Article 2, subparagraph 6, of the Labor Union Act, which is an actual practice of collective power. However, in actual practice it is difficult to differentiate between the occurrence of industrial disputes are taken for a certain period of time after the parties of the Labor Union Act apply for a mediation of the industrial dispute.

2. Industrial Actions

(1) Industrial Actions of the Labor Union Act

Industrial Actions refer to the struggles between the labor union and the employer to take advantage of the state of labor disputes in order to accomplish their goals. This shall not only contain "any controversy or difference arising from disagreements between a labor union and an employer with respect to the determination of conditions of employment", but also include "actions which obstruct the normal operations of a business".

Accordingly, industrial actions are such actions as strikes, sabotages, lockouts, and other activities to obstruct the normal operation of a business, but those actions such as assembling outside working hours or wearing ribbons are not industrial actions.

(2) Subject of industrial actions

The subject of industrial actions are the parties involved in the labor relationship. That is, the labor union represents the employees while the employer or employers' association represents the company.

(3) Purpose of industrial actions

The labor union is an organization that exists for the purpose of maintaining and improving their working conditions and enhancing their economic and social status. Accordingly, the main purpose of industrial actions is to maintain and improve working conditions. However, this is a narrow interpretation of the purpose. As an industrial action is a method used to accomplish means in a labor dispute, the purpose of industrial actions can be understood in respect to the contents of compulsory bargaining.

(4) Methods of industrial actions

Industrial actions are "actions which obstruct the normal operation of a business". Accordingly, those collective actions that do not obstruct the normal operation of a business, but intend to accomplish their means are not industrial actions. For example, wearing ribbons, sit-down strikes after working hours, etc. are not industrial actions.

Chapter 11

Intellectual Property

Section 1. Introduction

Intellectual property refers to creations of the mind: inventions, literary and artistic works, and symbols, names, and images used in commerce. Intellectual property is divided into two categories: Industrial property includes patents for inventions, trademarks, industrial designs and geographical indications. Copyright includes literary works such as novels, poems and plays, films, musical works, artistic works such as drawings, paintings, photographs and sculptures, and architectural designs. Rights related to copyrights include those of performing artists in their performances, producers of phonograms, and those of broadcasters in their radio and television programs.

1. Intellectual property rights

Intellectual property rights are like any other property rights - they allow the creator, or owner of a patent, trademark, or copyright, to benefit from his or her own work or investment. That is, these rights are rights to benefit from the protection of moral ad material interests resulting from authorship of any scientific, literary, or artistic production.

2. Reason to promote and protect intellectual property

There are several compelling reasons to promote and protect intellectual property. First, the progress and well-being of humanity rests on its capacity for new creations in the areas of technology and culture. Second, the legal protection of these new creations encourages the expenditure of additional resources, which leads to further innovation. Third, the promotion and protection of intellectual property spurs economic growth, creates new jobs and industries, and enhances the quality and enjoyment of life.

The intellectual property system helps strike a balance between the interests of the innovator and public interest, providing an environment in which creativity and invention can flourish for the benefit of all. Intellectual property rights reward creativity and human endeavor, which fuel the progress of humankind.

Section 2. Patent

A patent is an exclusive right granted for an invention, which is a product or process that provides a new way of doing something, or offers a new technical solution to a problem. A patent provides protection for the invention to the owner of the patent. The protection is granted for a limited period, 20 years from the date of filing an application.

1. Rights of patent owner

Patent protection means that the invention cannot be commercially made, used, distributed or sold without the patent owner's consent. These patent rights are enforced in a court, which hold the authority to stop patent infringement. Conversely, a court can also declare a patent invalid upon a successful challenge by a third party.

A patent owner has the right to decide who may - or may not - use the patented invention for the period in which the invention is protected. The patent owner may give permission or license to other parties to use the invention on mutually agreed terms. The owner may also sell the right to the invention to someone else, who will then become the new owner of the patent. Once a patent expires, the protection ends, and an invention enters the public domain, that is, the owner no longer holds exclusive rights to the invention, which becomes avaliable to commercial exploitation by others.

2. Theory for patent protection

Patents provide incentives to individuals by offering them recognition for their creativity and material reward for their marketable inventions. These incentives encourage innovation, which assures that the quality of human life is continuously enhanced. Patented inventions have, in fact, pervaded every aspect of human life, from electric lighting and plastic, to ball point pens and microprocessors.

All patent owners are obliged, in return for patent protection, to publicly disclose information on their invention in order to enrich the total body of technical knowledge in the world. Such an ever-increasing body of public knowledge promotes further creativity and innovation in others. In this way, patents provide not only protection for the owner but valuable information and inspiration for future generations of researchers and inventors.

3. Patenting process

The first step in securing a patent is the filing of a patent application. The patent application contains the title of the invention, as well as an indication of its technical field: it must include the background and a description of the invention, in clear language and in enough detail that an individual with average understanding of the field could use or reproduce the invention. Such descriptions are usually accompanied by visual materials such as drawings, plans, or diagrams to better describe the invention. The application also contains various claims, that is, information which determines the extent of protection granted by the patent.

A patent is granted by a national patent office (Korean Intellectual Property Office) after thorough examination of an application. The examination consists of two parts: a formality examination and a substantial examination. When a patent application is submitted to the office, it is checked to ensure that all requirements necessary to accord the application and filing date have been satisfied. The required information includes the name and address of an applicant, and power of attorney. If a document or information is missing, the office will issue a notice of amendment requesting the applicant to supplement the missing data within a specified time limit. If the applicant does not comply with such a request within the designated or extended period, the patent application will be nullified and then considered as having never been filed. The substantial examination mainly investigates subject matter of patent and patentability of the application required by Patent Act.

4. Subject matter of patents and patentability

An invention must fulfill the following conditions to be protected by a patent. It must be of industrial use: it must show an element of novelty, that is, some new characteristic that is not known in the body of existing knowledge in its technical field. This body of existing knowledge is called prior art. The invention must show an inventive step that could not be deduced by a person with average knowledge of the technical field. Finally, its subject matter must be accepted as patentable under law. Scientific theories, mathematical methods, discoveries of natural substances, commercial methods, or methods for medical treatment are not patentable.

Section 3. Trademark

A trademark is a distinctive sign, which identifies certain goods or services as those produced or provided by a specific person or enterprise. Its origin dates back to ancient times, when craftsmen reproduced their signatures, or marks on their artistic or utilitarian products. Over the years these marks evolved into today's system of trademark registration and protection. This system helps consumers identify and purchase a product or service because its nature and quality, indicated by unique trademark, meets their needs.

1. Function of trademarks

A trademark provides protection to the owner of a mark by ensuring the exclusive right to use it to identify goods or services, or to authorize another to use it in return for payment. The period of protection is 50 years from the registration date, but a trademark can be renewed indefinitely on payment of corresponding fees. Trademark protection is enforced by the courts, which have the authority to block trademark infringement.

In a large sense, trademarks promote initiative and enterprise by rewarding the owners of trademarks with recognition and financial profit. Trademark protection also hinders the effects of unfair competitors, such as counterfeiters, to use similar distinctive signs to market inferior or different products or services. The system enables people with skill and enterprise to produce and market goods and services in the fairest possible conditions, thereby facilitating international trade.

2. Subject matter

Trademarks may be one or a combination of words, letters, and numerals. They may consist of drawings, symbols, three-dimensional signs such as the shape and packaging of goods, or colors used as distinguishing features.

In addition to trademarks identifying the commercial source of goods and services, several other categories of marks exist. Collective marks are owned by an association whose members use them to identity themselves with a level of quality and other requirements set by the association. Examples of such associations would be those representing accountants, engineers, or architects. A business emblem is also protected under the Trademark Act. A business emblem refers to a mark used by a person engaged in a nonprofit business like YMCA or Boy Scouts to indicate that person's business.

3. Registration process

First, an application for registration of a trademark must be filed with the national trademark office (Korean Intellectual Property Office). The application must contain a clear reproduction of the sign filed for registration, including any colors, forms, or three-dimensional features. The application must also contain a list of goods or services to which the sign would apply. The sign must fulfill certain conditions in order to be protected as a trademark or other type of mark.

The trademark must be distinctive, so that consumers can distinguish it from other trademarks identifying other products, as well as identifying a particular product with it. It must neither mislead nor deceive customers or violate public order or morality. Finally, the rights applied for cannot be the same as, or similar to rights already granted to another trademark owner. This is determined through search and examination by the national office, or by the opposition of third parties who claim similar or identical rights.

4. Trademark right

National office maintains a Register of Trademarks, which contains full application information on all registrations and renewals, facilitating examination, search, and potential opposition by third parties. The effects of such a registration are limited to the country regionally.

Once a trademark is registered, a trademark right owner is entitled to exclusively use the registered trademark on the designated goods. Also, the owner may seek injunction against others who use any trademark, identical or similar to the registered trademark, and exercise a claim for infringement injunction or a right of compensation for damages against others who infringe the trademark right by using any trademark identical or similar to the registered mark.

Section 4. Industrial Design

An industrial design is the ornamental or aesthetic aspect of an article. The design may consist of three-dimensional features, such as the shape or surface of an article, or of two-dimensional features, such as patterns, lines or color.

Industrial designs are applied to a wide variety of products of industry and handicraft: from technical and medical instruments to watches, jewelry, and other luxury items; from housewares and electrical appliances to vehicles and architectural structures; from textile designs to leisure goods.

To be protected under the Industrial Design Act, an industrial design must be new or original and non-functional. This means that an industrial design is primarily of an aesthetic nature and any technical features of the article to which it is applied are not protected.

1. Reason to protect industrial design

Industrial designs are what make an article attractive and appealing: hence, they add to the commercial value of a product and increase its marketability. When an industrial design is protected, the owner - the person or entity that has registered the design - is assured an exclusive right against unauthorized copying or imitation of the design by third parties. This helps to ensure a fair return on investment. An effective system of protection also benefits consumers and the public at large, by promoting fair competition and honest trade practices, encouraging creativity, and promoting more aesthetically attractive products.

Protecting industrial designs helps economic development, by encouraging creativity in the industrial and manufacturing sectors, as well as in traditional arts and crafts. They contribute to the expansion of commercial activities and export of national products.

Industrial designs can be relatively simple and inexpensive to develop and protect. They are reasonably accessible to small and medium-sized enterprises as well as to individual artists and craftsmen.

2. Registration process

An industrial design must be registered in order to be protected under industrial design law. To be registerable, the design must be new or original. New means that no identical or very similar design is known to have existed before. Since protection of industrial design aims at economic development through encouraging the creativity of individuals, industrial applicability of article is also required. Industrial applicability refers to article with the same design that can be produced in large quantities by the industrial production methods. Here, industrial production methods include both mechanical and manual production methods.

Once a design is registered, a registration certificate is issued. Following that, the term of protection is 15 years from the date of registration. Industrial design protection is limited to the country in which protection is granted.

3. Design Right

Article 41 of the Industrial Design Act states that "The owner of design rights shall have the exclusive right to utilize the registered design and designs similar thereto commercially and industrially." The effect of design rights extend to similar designs as well since, if the design is limited to the same design, the scope of protection is extremely narrow and so its original purpose cannot be realized. The concept of similarity is defined as the scope by which the design has common homogeneity in its formative essence compared to the design represented in an article and so evokes a seemingly similar aesthetic sense.

Section 5. Copyright and Related Rights

Copyright is the body of laws which grants authors, artists and other creators protection for their literary and artistic creations. A closely associated field of rights related to copyright is "related rights", which provides rights similar or identical to those of copyright, although more limited and of shorter duration. The beneficiaries of related rights are performers, such as actors and musicians in their performances; producers of sound recordings in their recordings; and broadcasting organizations in their radio and television programs.

Works covered by copyright include, but are not limited to: novels, poems, plays, reference works, newspapers, computer programs, databases, films, musical compositions, choreography, paintings, drawings, photographs, sculpture, architecture, advertisements, maps, and technical drawings.

1. Exclusive rights

The creators of works protected by copyright, and their heirs and successors, have certain basic rights under copyright law. They hold the exclusive right to use or authorize others to use the works on agreed terms. The rights holder of a work can prohibit or authorize: its production in all form, including printing and sound recording, its public performance and communication to the public, its public performance and communication to the public, its broadcasting, its translation into other languages, and its adaptation, such as a novel into a screenplay for a film. Similar rights of, among other, fixation and reproduction are granted under related rights.

Many types of works protected under the law of copyright and related rights require mass distribution, communication, and financial investment for their successful dissemination; hence, creators often transfer the rights to their works to companies best able to develop and market the works, in return for compensation in the form of payments and/or royalties.

The economic rights of copyright have a duration, commencing upon the creation and fixation of the work, and lasting for 50 years after the creator's death. This term of protection enables both creators and their heirs and successors to benefit financially. Related rights enjoy short terms, 50 years after the performance, recording or broadcasting took place. Copyright and the protection of performers also include moral rights, which are the right to claim authorship of a work, and the right to oppose changes to the works which could harm the creator's reputation.

Rights provided for under copyright and related rights law can be enforced by rights holders through a variety of methods and fora, including by instituting civil actions, pursing administrative remedies, and through criminal prosecutions. Injunctions, orders requiring destruction of infringing items, and inspection orders are used to enforce rights.

2. Reason to protect copyright and related rights

Copyright and related rights protection is an essential component in fostering human creativity and innovation. Giving authors, artists and creators incentives in the form of recognition and fair economic rewards increases their activities and output and often enhances the results. Also, by insuring the existence and enforcement of rights, enterprises and companies can more easily invest in the creation, development, and global dissemination of works; this, in turn, helps increase access to, and enhances the enjoyment of, culture, knowledge, and entertainment all over the world, as well as stimulating economic and social development.

3. Protecting system of copyright and related rights

Copyright and related right protection is obtained automatically without any need for registration or other formalities. However, there is a national system of optional registration and deposit of works; this system facilitates, for example, questions involving disputes over ownership or creation, assignments and transfers of rights.

Many authors and performers do not have the ability or the means to pursue the legal and administrative enforcement of copyright and related rights, especially given the increasingly worldwide use of literary, musical and performance rights. As a result, the establishment and enhancement of collective management organizations and societies is a growing and necessary trend. These organizations can provide for their members the benefits of the organization's administrative and legal expertise and efficiency in, for example, collecting, managing, and disbursing royalties gained from national and international use of member's work or performance. Certain rights of producers of sound recordings and broadcasting organizations are sometimes managed collectively as well.

Chapter 12 The Marriage Institution

Section 1. Matrimonial Engagement

1. The meaning of matrimonial engagement

Matrimonial engagement is a contract between a man and a woman who are willing to contract a marriage. It is distinguished as separate from de facto marriage, in which marital life is enjoyed but not legally registered. It is also distinguished as separate from marriage, in which both the agreement to marry between the two parties and the marriage report have been registered.

2. The formation of matrimonial engagement

The matrimonial engagement is formed by agreement between t재 parties. To form the matrimonial engagement, both man and woman have to be eighteen years old or older. If a minor wants to enter into a matrimonial engagement, they should obtain the consent of both parents; if an incompetent wants to enter into a matrimonial engagement, he/she should obtain the consent of both parents or their guardian. And also, if a minor or an incompetent does not have a parent or guardian, or their parent or guardian is unable to give consent, they may enter into a matrimonial engagement with the consent of their family council.

3. The effect of matrimonial engagement

(1) Obligations of marriage

Once the matrimonial engagement has been formed, the parties have an obligation to contract the promised marriage at the appointed time. But in the case that anyone of the parties does not fulfill this obligation, the other person cannot claim to the court for compulsory performance of a matrimonial engagement. In this case, one party may claim against the other party who has breached the obligation only the damages therefrom. As for the scope of claims for damages, the negligent party shall be liable for damages from mental anguish in addition to property damages which were caused by the cancellation of an engagement.

(2) The infringement of matrimonial engagement by a third person

If a third person infringes on the matrimonial engagement during the contraction, he/she shall be bound to make compensation for damages arising therefrom. That is, if a third person committed adultery with a woman who was engaged to be married, and as a result caused the other party to dissolve the engagement, it can be said that the third person has infringed on the right of the man (the other party) with regard to the engagement. And naturally it causes him (the third person) the liability out of tort.

(3) Matrimonial engagement and the change of status relationship

Even though the parties (man and woman) have concluded matrimonial engagement, it creates no relative relations. Thus, even though a woman does give birth to a child during matrimonial engagement, it is regarded as a child out of wedlock. But, nonetheless, if the parties enter into marriage after the child was born, it becomes to a child in wedlock from then.

(4) The dissolution of matrimonial engagement

① The requisites

Because the matrimonial engagement is also a kind of contract related with status, it can be rescissible under certain conditions. The Article 804 of the Civil Act provides reasons for dissolution of matrimonial engagement as follows:

(a) If one of the parties has been sentenced to punishment of not less than suspension of qualification;

(b) If one of the parties has been identified as incompetent or quasi-incompetent after the conclusion of matrimonial engagement;

(c) If one of the parties has been suffering from venereal disease, incurable psychosis or any other incurable malignant disease;

(d) If one of the parties is engaged to or has married a person other than the party to the engagement after the conclusion of matrimonial engagement;

(e) If one of the parties has committed adultery with another person after the conclusion of matrimonial engagement;

(f) If the death and life of one of the parties has been unknown for one year or more after the conclusion of matrimonial engagement;

(g) If one of the parties has refused or delayed marriage without due reason; and

(h) If there exists any other serious reason.

② The method of dissolution of matrimonial engagement

Dissolution of matrimonial engagement shall be effected by the declaration of intention of one party to the other party. It is a unilateral act and only the parties of engagement can validly dissolve the matrimonial engagement. In cases where a party is unable to make any declaration of intention to the other party (i.e. disappearance, etc.), such engagement shall be deemed to have been dissolved when the cause of such dissolution becomes known to the dissolving party.

③ The effect

When a matrimonial engagement has been dissolved between parties, one party may claim against the other party in negligence the damages therefrom. As for the scope of claims for damages, the negligent party shall be liable for damages from mental anguish in addition to property damages.

Section 2. Marriage

1. The formation of marriage

In order to validly form a marriage, both formal and substantive requisites should be satisfied.

The substantive requisites are as follows: (1) The parties should mutually agree to the marriage; (2) both parties are at least 18 years of age; (3) if a minor wishes to marry, he/she should obtain the consent of both parents; (4) the marriage should not violate consanguineous marriage laws in Article 809 of the Civil Act; (5) the marriage should not violate bigamy laws in Article 810 of the Civil Act.

Next, as the formal requisite, the marriage should be reported in accordance with the provisions of the Act on the Registration and Others of Family Relationship. Therefore, a marriage without marriage report shall not be recognized as a legally valid marriage, although marital life is enjoyed substantively between the parties and the marital relationship is accepted in a social and customary sense.

2. The nullity and annulment of marriage

(1) The nullity of marriage

Even if a marriage report is submitted, a marriage can be null and void if it falls under any one of the following sub paragraphs:

① Where there is no agreement to marry between the parties;

② Where the marriage is in violation of Article 809 (1);

③ Where there exists or existed between the parties the relationship of lineal relatives by affinity; and

④ Where there existed between the parties the relationship of lineal blood relatives of adoptive parent line.

If the marriage be null and void, it cannot create any relative relations. Thus, in that case, even though a woman gives birth to a child during the marriage, it is regarded as not a child in wedlock but a child out of wedlock.

(2) The annulment of marriage

Even if a marriage is formed, it can be annulled under certain conditions. However, the annulment must be claimed only to the court and also the conciliation should be preceded before the claim (or action) for annulment, which is different from voidance in property law.

The causes for annulment of marriage under the Civil Act are as follows: ① a marriage in violation of marriageable age (Article 816, 817), ② a marriage without consent (Article 816, 819), ③ a consanguineous marriage (Article 816, 820), ④ bigamy (Article 816, 818), ⑤ a marriage due to malignant disease, etc. (Article 816, 822), ⑥ a marriage by fraud or duress (Article 816, 823).

3. The effect of marriage

(1) General effect

① The creation of relative relation

When a marriage is formed, husband and wife become relatives with each other as spouses. And also, to each one of the parties, a new relative relation by affinity has formed between each spouse and the spouse's blood relatives within the fourth degree of relationship or their spouses.

② Obligations to live together, to support and aid each other

Husband and wife shall live together, and shall support, and aid each other. The obligation (or duty) to live together means that husband and wife must determine the same place as a temporary domicile in which to reside. The meaning of living together is that husband and wife should live together not only as residers of the same space but also as a married couple. However, if they do not live together temporarily for a due reason, both parties must tolerate the separation.

③ Obligation to be faithful

Husband and wife should be faithful to each other. Therefore, if any one of the parties violates this obligation, it becomes the cause for a divorce.

④ Attaining majority by marriage

If a minor enters into marriage, he/she shall be deemed to have attained majority. This is called attaining majority by marriage. That is, the institution of attaining majority by marriage is a legislation which was enacted to enable a married minor enjoy his/her family life independently from the interference of a third party like an agent by law.

⑤ The right of representation for home affairs and the joint liability for obligations with respect to home affairs

Husband and wife shall exercise their rights of representation in relation to normal home affairs. This is what is called normal home affairs, meaning all affairs necessary for husband and wife to continue their cohabitation. It is difficult to describe uniformly what this consists of exactly because responsibilities differ by individual home communities. As a result, although the spouse has represented oneself (the principal) within the area of normal home affairs, the effect of that representation belongs to oneself (the principal).

⑥ Property relation with respect to marriage

The Civil Act provides a marital property system and a separate property system respectively in order to define property relations between husband and wife.

Although husband and wife are in a unitary and cooperative relationship in order to form or keep their cohabitation, each of them is respectively recognized as an independent actor regarding the property relations. Therefore, husband and wife may freely enter into a contract with respect to their property acquired during the marriage and their future marital property.

The separate property system is the system in which all property, pre-marital or marital, is owned separately. There occurred an important issue under this system. Among properties acquired during the marriage, which is presumed to be one's personal property and which is presumed to be under co-ownership? The Civil Act adopts the attitude of separation of goods. According to this, unless husband and wife have entered into a contract on marital property, any inherent property belonging to either husband or wife from the time before the marriage and any property acquired during the marriage in his or her own name are recognized as his or her peculiar property. Thus, husband and wife shall separately manage, use and take profit from these peculiar properties.

If properties are actually acquired by husband and wife's joint efforts, those properties are presumed to be in their co-ownership in spite of the name in the registration. And any property, of which title is uncertain between the husband and wife, shall be presumed to be in their co-ownership. Therefore, in the case of a divorce, those properties which are presumed to be in their co-ownership will become the object of claim for division of property.

Chapter 13

De Facto Marriage and Divorce

Section 1. *De Facto* Marriage (Common-law marriage)

1. Definition

A *de facto* marriage is a term used for those couples who live together but are not recognized by government authority because their marriage has not been reported.

2. The effect of *de facto* marriage

(1) The effect on status relationship

The provisions regarding the marital effect on status relationship are not applied to the *de facto* marriage. Thus, there occurs no relative relation between *de facto* spouses. And there occurs no affinity relation between any one of the party and the other's blood relatives as well. Also, a child born in a *de facto* marriage is regarded as a child out of wedlock, and when one of the parties dies, the other's right of inheritance is denied, too.

(2) The application of general effect of marriage

However, it is hard to deny that a *de facto* marriage also has similar qualities to a legal marriage. Thus, the provisions of the Civil Act which are related to general effects of marriage, such as the obligation to live together, to support and aid each other, the obligation to be faithful, the right of representation for home affairs, joint liability for obligations with respect to home affairs, etc. could be analogically applied to the de facto marriage. Also, when a *de facto* marriage is dissolved by causes attributable to any one of the parties or when a *de facto* marriage was infringed by a third person, the other party may claim the damages therefrom against the person in negligence or against the third person.

(3) The effect on property relation

Provisions regarding the obligation to jointly bear marital living expenses, the right of representation for normal home affairs, the joint liability for obligations with respect to home affairs, and peculiar property and property of which title is uncertain could also be analogically applied to the *de facto* marriage. Even the marital property system is possible between husband and wife of the *de facto* marriage, but the marital property system shall not be set up against a third person because it can not be validly registrated. As a result, the marital property system under the *de facto* marriage can be effective only between the two parties.

Section 2. Divorce

1. The extinction of marriage

(1) The meaning

The dissolution of marriage is the cancellation of a marriage that has previously been formed. There are two causes of the dissolution of marriage: the death of a spouse and divorce.

(2) Dissolution of marriage by the death of a spouse

If one of the parties dies, then the marital relation between husband and wife dissolves and the other spouse can remarry. Even though one of the parties dies, the affinity relatives between the surviving spouse and their spouse's blood relatives do not dissolve. But if the surviving spouse remarries, the blood relations with their previous in-laws shall be dissolved.

(3) Dissolution of marriage by divorce

① Divorce by agreement

Husband and wife may get a divorce by agreement and the causes of it need not to be inquired about. To form a divorce by agreement validly, both formal and substantive requisites together are required to be satisfied.

The substantive requisites are as follows: (a) The parties should mutually consent to the divorce; (b) If an incompetent wishes to divorce, he/she should obtain the consent of their parents or guardian. As a result, an incompetent may divorce by obtaining the consent of their parents or guardian, and if the incompetent does not have a parent or guardian, or their parent or guardian is unable to give consent, he/she may divorce with the consent of family council.

Next, the formal requisites are as follows: (a) (Counsel on divorce provided by the Family Court) To prevent divorce caused by sudden impulse, husband and wife who intend to get a divorce by agreement should have a counsel on divorce provided by the Family Court; (b) The careful deliberation period should have passed. The parties who have completed the counsel on divorce provided by the Family Court may confirm intention to divorce after three months if they have a child under their care, or after one month if they have no children under their care. The Family Court may exempt the party from or reduce the period described above when there are such urgent circumstances to proceed a divorce as the party's unbearable suffering due to domestic violence; (c) The parties who have a child to take care of submit the documents of agreement on fostering (under Article 837) and decision of custody (under Article 909 (4)) or the original copy of adjudication of the Family Court (under Article 837 and 909 (4)); (d) Husband and wife who have satisfied all the requisites described above may confirm intention to divorce to the Family Court at the place of the original address or at the place of address.

② The nullity and annulment of divorce by agreement

A divorce becomes null and void if there is no agreement to divorce between the parties. When the declaration of intent to divorce has been made by fraud or duress, the divorce can be annulled. The annulment must be claimed only to the court and no claim for annulment of a divorce by fraud or duress may be made, if three months have elapsed from the day when the party discovered the fraud, or became free from the duress.

③ Judicial divorce

Judicial divorce is the process with the aim to cancel marriage by litigation where there is no agreement to divorce between husband and wife, or when husband and wife are unable to agree with each other. In this case, in order to apply to the Family Court for a divorce, each case of the following causes for judicial divorce are required:

(a) One spouse must have committed an act of adultery.

(b) One spouse must have been maliciously deserted by the other spouse. Here, 'malicious desertion' means the unfulfillment of the obligation to live together, to support and aid each other, without any reasonable reason.

(c) One spouse must have been extremely maltreated by the other spouse or inlaws. Here, 'maltreatment' is defined as cruel behaviour on the body and the mind or the insult on one's honor. The 'extremely' is defined as the degree to which any one party cannot but stop the marital life because of their unbearable suffering.

(d) One spouse's lineal ascendant must have been extremely maltreated by the other spouse. Here, the meaning of 'maltreatment' is the same with the above.

(e) The death or life of the other spouse must have been unknown for three years or more.

(f) Or, any other difficult circumstances which make it difficult for one spouse to continue with the marriage.

2. The effect of divorce

(1) The effect on status relationship

If the marriage is cancelled, such status obligations between spouses, such as the obligation to remain faithful, the obligation to live together, to support and aid each other, is dissolved. Inlaw relations are also dissolved. Furthermore, it is natural that any one of the parties is able to remarry if they wish to. However, even though it is accepted that the inlaw relations are dissolved by divorce, it is prohibited for one of the divorced couple to marry with those people who had been their inlaws, such as spouses of blood relatives within the sixth degree of relationship, blood relatives of the spouse within the sixth degree of relationship, spouses of the blood relatives of the spouse within the fourth degree of relationship.

(2) The effect on children

A child born between husband and wife during marriage shall not lose their status as a child in wedlock after their parents are divorced. But if the child is a minor, he/she shall be necessary to choose who the person with parental authority is and who the custodian is between the divorced husband and wife. The reason for this is because it is difficult for both parents to equally exercise parental authority over the child after divorce.

① Decision on the person with parental authority of children

When parents are divorced, they can determine by agreement who the person with parental authority is. And if the parents fail to reach an agreement, the Family Court shall determine the person with parental authority upon the request of the parties.

② Decision on the custodian of children

After parents have divorced, they can determine by agreement matters concerning fostering their children. Where the agreement on fostering cannot or will not be made, the Family Court shall decide it upon a request of the party or ex officio matters related to fostering, taking consideration of children's intention and age, each parent's financial status and other circumstances.

③ Decision on custodian by the Family Court

When parents are divorced, the agreement on matters concerning fostering their children shall include matters as follows:

(a) Decision on the custodian;
(b) Child support; and
(c) Visitation right and methods thereof.

But, in spite of the agreement determined above, the Family Court may change matters concerning fostering or take other appropriate measures, upon a request of each parent, children or public prosecutor or ex officio where it is deemed necessary for children's welfare.

④ The visitation right

The visitation right is the right granted by a court to either parent (or other relative) who is deprived of custody of a child and the child itself to visit or to contact by calls, letters, etc. each other on a regular basis. That is, a parent who does not have custody of their children are granted the visitation right.

(3) The effect on property relation

① Right to claim for damages

In case of a judicial divorce, any one of the parties who causes losses to or inflicts injuries on the other party willfully or negligently, shall be bound to make compensation for damages arising therefrom. As for the scope of claims for damages, the negligent party shall be liable for damages from mental anguish in addition to property damages.

② Claim for division of property

The objects of claim for division of property are the properties which are acquired by husband and wife's joint efforts during the marriage and thus which are presumed to be in their co-ownership. Inherent property belonging to either husband or wife from the time before the marriage, and property acquired during the marriage in his or her own name shall constitute his or her peculiar property, which is not the object of claim for division in principle. But even in case of the peculiar property, if the other party had specially contributed to the maintenance of the property and, as a result, prevented the property loss, then it could be the object of claim for division of property.

Regarding remedy for infringements on claim for division of property, when a party files a legal action for a property right, knowing that such action may obstruct the other party's exercise of a claim for division of property, the other party may file a lawsuit demanding a revocation of such action and recovery therefrom with the Family Court. The action must be brought to court within one year from the time when the other party became aware of the cause for revocation, or within five years from the time when the juristic action occurred.

Chapter 14 International Law

Section 1. International Relations
Section 2. Status of Foreigners

Section 1. International Relations

1. Concept of international law

International law governs relations between nations internationally according to agreements of members. Nations are the subject of rights and duties in international law, and international organizations and private persons are also the subject with some limitations set by each state of members.

2. International law and domestic law

(1) International law and domestic law

Nowadays, the distinction between international law and domestic law becomes unclear in many cases owing to the extension of jurisdiction and subject matters. Therefore, problems to be solved appear in conflict between different legal systems and between international law and domestic law.

(2) Theory for the relation between international law and domestic law

① Theory for superiority of domestic law

Theory for superiority of domestic law originated from the extreme nationalism of Germany during the 18th and 19th centuries. The theory emphasizes absolute sovereignty of each nation, and denies international law as a result. According to the theory, domestic law consists of interior and exterior law which, in turn, constitute singular legal order. Hence, international law as a legal order is denied since it is merely exteriority of domestic law.

② Theory for superiority of international law

Theory for superiority of international law was developed under the influence of structuring international societies and constructing international orders boomingly. The theory asserts that domestic law is just a part of legal order authorized by international law. International law thus is justified in the sense that it mandates domestic law. The theory is prevalent today, and is conformable to international pacifism. However, there is no international law which has authority to order domestic law for complying with otherwise to nullify.

3. Nation

The sovereignty of a nation is the highest power within the nation and an indication of independence internationally. The sovereignty authorizes the nation with the highest power to govern its own people and its territory. The nation can force its people to obey an order, and has authority to dispose of its property as well. The nation has no right for other nations, and of course other nations shall respect such rule.

(1) National territory

The nation has an exclusive right to govern the national territory with a limitation set by an international law. Such territorial right consists of dominium, which is a right to use, make profits, or dispose of the territory, and imperium, which is a right to govern freely within the territory. The national territory is constituted by territorial land, sea and air.

① Territorial land

Territorial land, which is the most important part of the national territory, includes land and islands of the nation. All inland waters, lakes, and canals are included in territorial land. The nation has also a right to control the surface of the land as well as the underground inside the border line. The nation has an exclusive jurisdiction on its territorial land, unlike territorial sea or air.

② Territorial sea (Territorial waters)

Territorial sea is defined by all waters seaward to a certain distance from the coastline, and thus the width of the territorial sea is denoted by a distance from the baseline. There are two ways to decide the width of the territorial sea; normal baseline and straight baseline. The normal baseline is the low-water line along the coast as marked on large-scale charts officially recognized by the coastal state. Alternatively straight baseline can be defined connecting fringing islands along a coast, across the mouths of rivers, or with certain restrictions across the mouths of bays. The straight baseline is useful in cases where the coastline is winding or there are many islands and reefs near the coastline.

③ Territorial air (Airspace)

Airspace means the portion of the atmosphere controlled by a country above its territory, including its territorial waters. Unlike the territorial waters, no navigation of foreign-flag airplanes is allowed in the airspace where the nation exerts exclusive authority. There is no international agreement on the vertical extent of sovereign airspace except the border of outer space. This is an recent issue to be solved in international society since nations around the world have conflict interests over space.

4. Law of the Sea Convention

The United Nations Convention on the Law of the Sea is the international agreement that resulted from discussions to ease conflict interests over sea between developed countries and undeveloped countries. This treaty came into force from November sixteenth, 1994, and is called the Constitution of the Sea.

The convention sets the limit of various areas, such as 12 nautical miles rule for territorial waters, 24 nautical miles rule for contiguous zone, 200 nautical miles rule for exclusive economic zone, and the continental shelf. Aside from its provisions defining ocean boundaries, the convention establishes general obligations for safeguarding the marine environment and protecting freedom of scientific research on the high seas, and also creates an innovative legal regime for controlling mineral resource exploitation in deep seabed areas beyond national jurisdiction, through the International Seabed Authority and the Common Heritage of Mankind Principle. The International Tribunal for the law of the Sea is an intergovernmental organization created by the United Nations Convention on the Law of the Sea to settle disputes between state parties.

(1) Continental shelf

The continental shelf is defined as the natural prolongation of the land territory to the continental margin's outer edge, or 200 nautical miles from the coastal state's baseline, whichever is greater. Coastal states have the right to harvest mineral and non-living material in the subsoil of its continental shelf, to the exclusion of others. Coastal states also have exclusive control over living resources attached to the continental shelf, but not to creatures living in the water column beyond the exclusive economic zone.

5. International Organization

(1) Privilege for the chief of state

According to international law, the chief of state has certain kinds of privileges and immunities during official or unofficial visits of foreign countries. During official visits by mutual consent, the privileges and immunities are extensive over a vast ranged area. All of the family members and attendants also have such privileges and immunities as well as exemption from civil and criminal jurisdiction.

(2) Diplomats

① Duty of diplomats

A diplomat is a person appointed by a state to conduct diplomacy with another state or international organization. Therefore, a diplomat represents the sending nation and protects its interests through negotiations. Also, a diplomat collects and reports information that could affect national interests. Duties of the diplomat include the promotion of friendly relations with collaborations in economic, scientific, and cultural areas. The accepting state has to provide all conveniences for a diplomat to carry out his/her duty.

② Diplomatic privileges and immunities

A diplomat is entitled to have privileges and immunities to carry out his/her duty by representing the sending state with dignity. Such diplomatic privileges are inviolability and extraterritoriality.

③ Consuls

A consul represents his/her state in a number of administrative ways, but doesn't have the diplomat's political functions. Duties of consuls includes to assist and protect the citizens of the sending state, to facilitate trade and friendship between the people of the sending state and the accredited state, to provide assistance with bureaucratic issues, to protect inheritable rights of citizens of the sending state, to be an agency for a citizen of the sending state, to provide legal advice for citizens of the sending state, and to supervise airplanes and ships of the sending state. A consul also has diplomatic privileges such as extraterritoriality.

Section 2. Status of Foreigners

1. Rights of foreigners

A human being is entitled to have equal rights for human dignity and worth regardless of nationality, religion, culture, language, and personal ability.

(1) Rights which shall not be denied for foreigners

All fundamental rights and equal protection of law are guaranteed for both resident aliens and non-resident aliens.

(2) Rights which shall be awarded to foreigners

Rights which shall be awarded to foreigners include the right of due process, freedom of religion, freedom of family life, freedom of expression, freedom of assembly and association, property right, social security right, the right to strike, the right to leave a country, and the right to move at will within the borderline. These rights can be restricted when there are enough reasons to justify.

(3) Rights which shall not be awarded to foreigners

Rights which shall not be awarded to foreigners include the right to move freely beyond the borderline, political right, proprietary right, and economic right. Some states recognize some of these rights such as right to enter residential state, political rights concerned only with domestic matters and economic rights under domestic laws or bilateral treaties. To move forward internationally with mutual understanding and development, protections for minorities and foreigners must be upgraded further.

2. Right to protect in abroad

Right to protect in abroad enables a country to request an assaulting state to provide remedies for citizens who reside in the assaulting state and receive unfair treatment or infringement of rights. This right originated from the sovereignty of state, and is not an exercise of procuration. The homeland shall not exercise this right unless an infringed citizen already requests remedies under the law of residing state. This principle is designed to avoid international disputes caused by civil disputes, and this right can be restricted when members of a treaty have an agreement.

3. Extradition

Extradition is the official process whereby a nation or state surrenders a suspected or convicted criminal to another nation or state. The consensus in international law is that a state does not have any obligation to surrender an alleged criminal to foreign state as one principle of sovereignty is that every state has legal authority over the people within its borders. Such absence of international obligation and the desire of the right to demand such criminals of other countries have caused a web of extradition treaties or agreements to evolve; most countries in the world have signed bilateral extradition treaties with most other countries. Reasons for extradition are the following. The best place for trial, adjudication, and resultant penalty is the place where a crime occurred; Since requirements for conviction are quite similar in most of countries, extradition is an effective way to reduce crimes for both requesting country and surrendering country.

Annex

CONSTITUTION OF THE REPUBLIC OF KOREA

CHAPTER Ⅰ GENERAL PROVISIONS

Article 1

(1) The Republic of Korea shall be a democratic republic.

(2) The sovereignty of the Republic of Korea shall reside in the people and all states.

Article 2

(1) Nationality of the people of the Republic of Korea shall be prescribed by Act.

(2) It shall be the duty of the State to protect citizens residing abroad as prescribed by Act.

Article 3

The territory of the Republic of Korea shall consist of the Korean peninsula and its adjacent islands.

Article 4

The Republic of Korea shall seek unification and shall formulate and carry out a policy of peaceful unification based on the principles of freedom and democracy.

Article 5

(1) The Republic of Korea shall endeavor to maintain international peace and shall renounce all aggressive wars.

(2) The Armed Forces shall be charged with the sacred mission of national security and defense of the land and their political neutrality shall be maintained.

Article 6

(1) Treaties duly concluded and promulgated under the Constitution and the generally recognized rules of international law shall have the

same effect as the domestic laws of the Republic of Korea.

(2) The status of aliens shall be guaranteed as prescribed by international law and treaties.

Article 7

(1) All public officials shall be servants of the people and shall be responsible to the people.

(2) The status and political impartiality of public officials shall be guaranteed as prescribed by Act.

Article 8

(1) The establishment of political parties shall be free and the plural party system shall be guaranteed.

(2) Political parties shall be democratic in their objectives, organization, and activities and shall have the necessary organizational arrangements for the people to participate in the formation of the political will.

(3) Political parties shall enjoy the protection of the State and may be provided with operational funds by the State under the conditions as prescribed by Act.

(4) If the purposes or activities of a political party are contrary to the fundamental democratic order, the Government may bring an action against it in the Constitutional Court for its dissolution, and the political party shall be dissolved in accordance with the decision of the Constitutional Court.

Article 9

The State shall strive to sustain and develop its cultural heritage and to enhance its national culture.

CHAPTER II RIGHTS AND DUTIES OF CITIZENS

Article 10

All citizens shall be assured of their human worth and dignity and shall have the right to pursue happiness. It shall be the duty of the State to confirm and guarantee the fundamental and inviolable human rights of individuals.

Article 11

(1) All citizens shall be equal before the law and there shall be no discrimination in political, economic, social, or cultural life on account of sex, religion, or social status.

(2) No privileged caste shall be recognized nor established in any form.

(3) The awarding of decorations or distinctions of honor in any form shall be effective only for recipients and no privileges shall ensue therefrom.

Article 12

(1) All citizens shall enjoy personal liberty. No person shall be arrested, detained, searched, seized, or interrogated except as provided by Act. No person shall be punished, placed under preventive restrictions or be subjected to involuntary labor except as provided by Act and through lawful procedures.

(2) No citizen shall be tortured or be compelled to testify against himself in criminal cases.

(3) Warrants issued by a judge through due procedures upon the request of a prosecutor shall be presented in case of arrest, detention, seizure or search. Provided, that in a case where a criminal suspect is apprehended while in the very act of committing an offense or where there is danger that a person suspected of committing a crime punishable by imprisonment of three years or more may escape or destroy evidence, then investigative authorities may request an ex post facto warrant.

(4) Any person who is arrested or detained shall have the right to prompt assistance of counsel. When a criminal defendant is unable to secure counsel by his own efforts, the State shall assign counsel for the defendant as prescribed by Act.

(5) No person shall be arrested or detained without being informed of the reason thereof and of his right to assistance of counsel. The family, etc., as designated by Act, of a person arrested or detained shall be notified without delay of the reason for and the time and place of the arrest or detention.
(6) Any person who is arrested or detained shall have the right to request the court to review the legality of the arrest or detention.
(7) In a case where a confession is deemed to have been made against the will of a defendant due to torture, violence, intimidation, unduly prolonged arrest, deceit or in a case where a confession is the only evidence against a defendant in a formal trial, such a confession shall not be admitted as evidence of guilt, nor shall a defendant be punished by reason of such a confession.

Article 13

(1) No citizen shall be prosecuted for an act which does not constitute a crime under an Act in force at the time it was committed, nor shall he be placed in double jeopardy.
(2) No restriction shall be imposed upon the political rights of any citizen, nor shall any person be deprived of property rights by means of retroactive legislation.
(3) No citizen shall suffer unfavorable treatment on account of an act not of his own doing but committed by a relative.

Article 14

All citizens shall enjoy freedom of residence and the right to move at will.

Article 15

All citizens shall enjoy freedom of occupation.

Article 16

All citizens shall be free from intrusion into their place of residence. In case of search or seizure in a residence, a warrant issued by a judge upon request of a prosecutor shall be presented.

Article 17

The right to privacy of all citizens shall not be infringed.

Article 18

The privacy of correspondence of all citizens shall not be infringed.

Article 19

All citizens shall enjoy freedom of conscience.

Article 20

(1) All citizens shall enjoy freedom of religion.

(2) No state religion shall be recognized and there should be a separation of the state and of religion.

Article 21

(1) All citizens shall enjoy the freedom of speech and of the press and the freedom of assembly and of association.

(2) Licensing or censorship of speech and the press and licensing of assembly and association shall not be recognized.

(3) The standards of news service and broadcast facilities and matters necessary to ensure the functions of newspapers shall be determined by Act.

(4) Neither speech nor the press shall violate the honor or rights of other persons nor undermine public morals or social ethics. Should speech or the press violate the honor or rights of other persons, claims may be made for the damage resulting therefrom.

Article 22

(1) All citizens shall enjoy the freedom of learning and the arts.

(2) The rights of authors, inventors, scientists, engineers, and artists shall be protected by Act.

Article 23

(1) The right of property of all citizens shall be guaranteed. The contents

and limitations thereof shall be determined by Act.
(2) The exercise of property rights shall conform to the public welfare.
(3) Expropriation, use or restriction of private property from public necessity and compensation there for shall be governed by Act. Provided, that in such a case, just compensation shall be paid.

Article 24

All citizens shall have the right to vote under the conditions as prescribed by Act.

Article 25

All citizens shall have the right to hold public office under the conditions as prescribed by Act.

Article 26

(1) All citizens shall have the right to petition in writing to any governmental agency under the conditions as prescribed by Act.
(2) The State shall be obligated to examine all such petitions.

Article 27

(1) All citizens shall have the right to be tried in conformity with the Act by judges qualified under the Constitution and the Act.
(2) Citizens who are not on active military service or who are not employees of the military forces shall not be tried by a court martial within the territory of the Republic of Korea, except in case of crimes as prescribed by Act involving important classified military information, sentinels, sentry posts, the supply of harmful food and beverages, prisoners of war and military Articles and facilities and in the case of a proclamation of extraordinary martial law.
(3) All citizens shall have the right to a speedy trial. The accused shall have the right to a public trial without delay in the absence of justifiable reasons to the contrary.
(4) The accused shall be presumed innocent until a judgment of guilt has

been pronounced.

(5) A victim of a crime shall be entitled to make a statement during the proceedings of the trial of the case involved as under the conditions prescribed by Act.

Article 28

In a case where a criminal suspect or an accused person who has been placed under detention is not indicted as provided by Act or is acquitted by a court, he shall be entitled to claim just compensation from the State under the conditions as prescribed by Act.

Article 29

(1) In case a person has sustained damages by an unlawful act committed by a public official in the course of official duties, he may claim just compensation from the State or public organization under the conditions as prescribed by Act. In this case, the public official concerned shall not be immune from liabilities.

(2) In case a person on active military service, an employee of the military forces, a police official, or others as prescribed by Act sustains damages in connection with the performance of official duties such as combat action, drill and so forth, he shall not be entitled to a claim against the State or public organization on the ground of unlawful acts committed by public officials in the course of official duties, but shall be entitled only to compensations as prescribed by Act.

Article 30

Citizens who have suffered bodily injury or death due to criminal acts of others may receive aid from the State under the conditions as prescribed by Act.

Article 31

(1) All citizens shall have an equal right to receive an education correspond-

ing to their abilities.

(2) All citizens who have children to support shall be responsible at least for their elementary education and other education as provided by Act.

(3) Compulsory education shall be free of charge.

(4) Independence, professionalism, and political impartiality of education and the autonomy of institutions of higher learning shall be guaranteed under the conditions as prescribed by Act.

(5) The State shall promote lifelong education.

(6) Fundamental matters pertaining to the educational system, including in-school and lifelong education, administration, finance, and the status of teachers shall be determined by Act.

Article 32

(1) All citizens shall have the right to work. The State shall endeavor to promote the employment of workers and to guarantee optimum wages through social and economic means and shall enforce a minimum wage system under the conditions as prescribed by Act.

(2) All citizens shall have the duty to work. The State shall prescribe by Act the extent and conditions of the duty to work in conformity with democratic principles.

(3) Standards of working conditions shall be determined by Act in such a way as to guarantee human dignity.

(4) Special protection shall be accorded to working women and they shall not be subjected to unjust discrimination in terms of employment, wages, and working conditions.

(5) Special protection shall be accorded to working children.

(6) The opportunity to work shall be accorded preferentially, under the conditions as prescribed by Act, to those who have given distinguished service to the State, wounded veterans and policemen, and members of the bereaved

families of military servicemen and policemen killed in action.

Article 33

(1) To enhance working conditions, workers shall have the right to independent association, collective bargaining, and collective action.

(2) Only those public officials, who are designated by Act, shall have the right to association, collective bargaining, and collective action.

(3) The right to collective action of workers employed by important defense industries may be either restricted or denied under the conditions as prescribed by Act.

Article 34

(1) All citizens shall be entitled to a life worthy of human beings.

(2) The State shall have the duty to endeavor to promote social security and welfare.

(3) The State shall endeavor to promote the welfare and rights of women.

(4) The State shall have the duty to implement policies for enhancing the welfare of senior citizens and the minors.

(5) Citizens who are incapable of earning a livelihood due to a physical disability, disease, old age, or other reasons shall be protected by the State under the conditions as prescribed by Act.

(6) The State shall endeavor to prevent disasters and to protect citizens from harm therefrom.

Article 35

(1) All citizens shall have the right to a healthy and pleasant environment. The State and all citizens shall endeavor to protect the environment.

(2) The substance of the environmental right shall be determined by Act.

(3)The State shall endeavor to ensure comfortable housing for all citizens through housing development policies and the like.

Article 36

(1) Marriage and family life shall be entered into and sustained on the basis of individual dignity and equality of the sexes, and the State shall do everything in its power to achieve that goal.
(2) The State shall endeavor to protect mothers.
(3) The health of all citizens shall be protected by the State.

Article 37

(1) Freedoms and rights of citizens shall not be neglected on the ground that they are not enumerated in the Constitution.
(2) The freedoms and rights of citizens may be restricted by Act only when necessary for national security, the maintenance of law and order, or for public welfare. Even when such restriction is imposed, no essential aspect of the freedom or right shall be violated.

Article 38

All citizens shall have the duty to pay taxes under the conditions as prescribed by Act.

Article 39

(1) All citizens shall have the duty of national defense under the conditions as prescribed by Act.
(2) No citizen shall be treated unfavorably on account of the fulfillment of his obligation of military service.

CHAPTER Ⅲ THE NATIONAL ASSEMBLY

Article 40

The legislative power shall be vested in the National Assembly.

Article 41

(1) The National Assembly shall be composed of members elected by universal, equal, direct, and secret ballot by the citizens.

(2) The number of members of the National Assembly shall be determined by Act, but the number shall not be less than 200.
(3) The constituencies of members of the National Assembly, proportional representation, and other matters pertaining to National Assembly elections shall be determined by Act.

Article 42

The term of office of members of the National Assembly shall be four years.

Article 43

Members of the National Assembly shall not concurrently hold any other office prescribed by Act.

Article 44

(1) During the sessions of the National Assembly, no member of the National Assembly shall be arrested or detained without the consent of the National Assembly except in case the member is in the very act of committing an offense.
(2) In case of apprehension or detention of a member of the National Assembly prior to the opening of a session, such member shall be released during the session upon the request of the National Assembly, except when the member is apprehended and detained while in the very act of committing an offense.

Article 45

No member of the National Assembly shall be held responsible outside the National Assembly for opinions officially expressed or votes cast in the Assembly.

Article 46

(1) Members of the National Assembly shall have the duty to maintain high standards of integrity.
(2) Members of the National Assembly shall give preference to national in-

terests and shall perform their duties in accordance with their conscience.
(3) Members of the National Assembly shall not acquire, through abuse of their positions, rights, and interests in property or positions, or assist other persons to acquire the same, by means of contracts with or dispositions by the State, public organizations, or industries.

Article 47

(1) A regular session of the National Assembly shall be convened once every year under the conditions as prescribed by Act and extraordinary sessions of the National Assembly shall be convened upon the request of the President or one fourth or more of the total members.
(2) The period of regular sessions shall not exceed a hundred days, and that of extraordinary sessions, thirty days.
(3) If the President requests the convening of an extraordinary session, the period of the session and the reasons for the request shall be clearly specified.

Article 48

The National Assembly shall elect one Speaker and two Vice-Speakers.

Article 49

Except as otherwise provided for in the Constitution or in Act, the attendance of a majority of the total members, and the concurrent vote of a majority of the members present, shall be necessary for decisions of the National Assembly. In case of a tie vote, the matter shall be regarded as rejected.

Article 50

(1) Sessions of the National Assembly shall be open to the public. Provided, that when it is decided so by a majority of the members present or when the Speaker deems it necessary to do so for the sake of national security, they may be closed to the public.

(2) The public disclosure of the proceedings of sessions which were not open to the public shall be determined by Act.

Article 51

Bills and other matters submitted to the National Assembly for deliberation shall not be abandoned on the ground that they were not acted upon during the session in which they were introduced, except in a case where the term of the members of the National Assembly has expired.

Article 52

Bills may be introduced by members of the National Assembly or by the Executive.

Article 53

(1) Each bill passed by the National Assembly shall be sent to the Executive, and the President shall promulgate it within fifteen days.

(2) In case of objection to a bill, the President may, within the period referred to in paragraph (1), return it to the National Assembly with written explanation of his objection, and request it be reconsidered. The President may do the same during adjournment of the National Assembly.

(3) The President shall not request the National Assembly to reconsider a bill in part, or with proposed amendments.

(4) In case there is a request for reconsideration of a bill, the National Assembly shall reconsider it, and if the National Assembly again passes the bill in the original form with the attendance of more than one half of the total members, and with a concurrent vote of two thirds or more of the members present, it shall become Act.

(5) If the President does not promulgate a bill, or does not request the National Assembly to reconsider it within the period referred to in paragraph (1), it shall become Act.

(6) The President shall promulgate without delay an Act as finalized under

paragraphs (4) and (5). If the President does not promulgate an Act within five days after it has become Act under paragraph (5), or after it has been returned to the Executive under paragraph (4), the Speaker shall promulgate it.

(7) Except as provided otherwise, an Act shall take effect twenty days after the date of promulgation.

Article 54

(1) The National Assembly shall deliberate and decide upon the national budget bill.

(2) The Executive shall formulate the budget bill for each fiscal year and submit it to the National Assembly within ninety days before the beginning of a fiscal year. The National Assembly shall decide upon it within thirty days before the beginning of the fiscal year.

(3) If the budget bill is not passed by the beginning of the fiscal year, the Executive may, in conformity with the budget of the previous fiscal year, disburse funds for the following purposes until the budget bill is passed by the National Assembly:

1. The maintenance and operation of agencies and facilities established by the Constitution or by Act;
2. Execution of the obligatory expenditures as prescribed by Act; and
3. Continuation of projects previously approved in the budget.

Article 55

(1) In a case where it is necessary to make continuing disbursements for a period longer than one fiscal year, the Executive shall obtain the approval of the National Assembly for a specified period of time.

(2) A reserve fund shall be approved by the National Assembly in its totality. The disbursement of the reserve fund shall be approved during the next session of the National Assembly.

Article 56

When it is necessary to amend the budget, the Executive may formulate a supplementary revised budget bill and submit it to the National Assembly.

Article 57

The National Assembly shall not, without the consent of the Executive, increase the sum of any item of expenditure or create any new items of expenditure in the budget submitted by the Executive.

Article 58

When the Executive plans to issue national bonds or to conclude contracts which may incur financial obligations on the State outside the budget, it shall have the prior concurrence of the National Assembly.

Article 59

Types and rates of taxes shall be determined by Act.

Article 60

(1) The National Assembly shall have the right to consent to the conclusion and ratification of treaties pertaining to mutual assistance or mutual security; treaties concerning important international organizations; treaties of friendship, trade, and navigation; treaties pertaining to any restriction in sovereignty; peace treaties; treaties which will burden the State or people with an important financial obligation; or treaties related to legislative matters.

(2) The National Assembly shall also have the right to consent to the declaration of war, the dispatch of armed forces to foreign states, or the stationing of alien forces in the territory of the Republic of Korea.

Article 61

(1) The National Assembly may inspect affairs of the state or investigate specific matters of state affairs and may demand the production of documents directly related thereto, the appearance of a witness in person, and the furnishing of testimony or statements of opinion.

(2) The procedures and other necessary matters concerning the inspection and investigation of state administration shall be determined by Act.

Article 62

(1) The Prime Minister, members of the State Council, or government delegates may attend meetings of the National Assembly or its committees and report on the state administration or deliver opinions and answer questions.

(2) When requested by the National Assembly or its committees, the Prime Minister, members of the State Council or government delegates shall attend any meeting of the National Assembly and answer questions. If the Prime Minister or State Council members are requested to attend, the Prime Minister or State Council members may have State Council members or government delegates attend any meeting of the National Assembly and answer questions.

Article 63

(1) The National Assembly may pass a recommendation for the removal of the Prime Minister or a State Council member from office.

(2) A recommendation for removal as referred to in paragraph (1) may be introduced by one third or more of the total members of the National Assembly, and shall be passed with the concurrent vote of a majority of the total members of the National Assembly.

Article 64

(1) The National Assembly may establish the rules of its proceedings and internal regulations. Provided, that they are not in conflict with an Act.

(2) The National Assembly may review the qualifications of its members and may take disciplinary actions against its members.

(3) The concurrent vote of two thirds or more of the total members of the National Assembly shall be required for the expulsion of any member. (4)No action shall be brought to court with regard to decisions taken under para-

graphs (2) and (3).

Article 65

(1) In case the President, the Prime Minister, members of the State Council, heads of Executive Ministries, Justices of the Constitutional Court, judges, members of the National Election Commission, the Chairman and members of the Board of Audit and Inspection, and other public officials designated by Act have violated the Constitution or other Acts in the performance of official duties, the National Assembly may pass motions for their impeachment.

(2) A motion for impeachment prescribed in paragraph (1) may be proposed by one third or more of the total members of the National Assembly, and shall require a concurrent vote of a majority of the total members of the National Assembly for passage. Provided, that a motion for the impeachment of the President shall be proposed by a majority of the total members of the National Assembly and approved by two thirds or more of the total members of the National Assembly. (3) Any person against whom a motion for impeachment has been passed shall be suspended from exercising his power until the impeachment has been adjudicated.

(4) A decision on impeachment shall not extend further than removal from public office. Provided, that it shall not exempt the person impeached from civil or criminal liability.

CHAPTER Ⅳ THE EXECUTIVE

SECTION 1 The President

Article 66

(1) The President shall be the Head of State and shall represent the State

vis-a-vis foreign states.

(2) The President shall have the responsibility and duty to safeguard the independence, territorial integrity, and continuity of the State and the Constitution.

(3) The President shall have the duty to sincerely pursue the peaceful unification of the homeland.

(4) Executive power shall be vested in the Executive Branch headed by the President.

Article 67

(1) The President shall be elected by universal, equal, direct, and secret ballot by the people.

(2) In case two or more persons receive the same largest number of votes in the election as referred to in paragraph (1), the person who receives the largest number of votes in an open session of the National Assembly attended by a majority of the total members of the National Assembly shall be elected.

(3) If and when there is only one presidential candidate, he shall not be elected President unless he receives at least one third of the total eligible votes.

(4) Citizens who are eligible for election to the National Assembly, and who have reached the age of forty years or more on the date of the presidential election, shall be eligible to be elected to the presidency.

(5) Matters pertaining to presidential elections shall be determined by Act.

Article 68

(1) The successor to the incumbent President shall be elected forty to seventy days before his term expires.

(2) In case a vacancy occurs in the office of the President, or the President-elect dies, or is disqualified by a court ruling or for any other rea-

son, a successor shall be elected within sixty days from the date when the vacancy, death, or disqualification occurs.

Article 69

The President, at the time of his inauguration, shall take the following oath: "I do solemnly swear before the people that I will faithfully execute the duties of the President by observing the Constitution, defending the State, pursuing the peaceful unification of the homeland, promoting the freedom and welfare of the people and endeavoring to develop national culture."

Article 70

The term of the office of the President shall be five years, without reelection.

Article 71

If the Office of the President is vacant or the President is unable to perform his duties for any reason, the Prime Minister or the members of the State Council in the order of priority as determined by Act, shall act for him.

Article 72

The President may submit important policies relating to diplomacy, national defense, unification, and other matters relating to the national destiny to a national referendum if he deems it necessary.

Article 73

The President shall conclude and ratify treaties; accredit, receive or dispatch diplomatic envoys; and declare war and conclude peace.

Article 74

(1) The President shall be Commander-in-Chief of the Armed Forces under the conditions as prescribed by the Constitution and by Act.

(2)The organization and formation of the Armed Forces shall be determined by Act.

Article 75

The President may issue presidential decrees concerning matters delegated to him by Act with the scope specifically defined and also matters necessary to enforce Acts.

Article 76

(1) In time of internal turmoil, external menace, natural calamity, or a grave financial or economic crisis, the President may take the minimum necessary financial and economic actions or issue orders having the effect of Act, only when it is required to take urgent measures for the maintenance of national security or public peace and order, and there is no time to await the convocation of the National Assembly.

(2) In case of major hostilities affecting national security, the President may issue orders having the effect of Act, only when it is required to preserve the integrity of the nation, and it is impossible to convene the National Assembly.

(3) In case actions taken or orders issued under paragraphs (1) and (2), the President shall promptly notify the National Assembly and obtain its approval.

(4) In case no approval is obtained, the actions or orders shall lose its effect. In such case, the Acts which were amended or abolished by the orders in question shall automatically regain their original effect from the moment the orders fail to obtain approval.

(5) The President shall, without delay, make public notice developments under paragraphs (3) and (4).

Article 77

(1) When the President required to cope with a military necessity or to maintain the public safety and order by mobilization of the military forces in time of war, armed conflict, or similar national emergency, he may proclaim martial law under the conditions as prescribed by Act.

(2) Martial law shall be of two types: extraordinary martial law and precautionary martial law.
(3) Under extraordinary martial law, special measures may be taken with respect to the necessity for warrants, freedom of speech, the press, assembly and association, or the powers of the Executive and the Judiciary under the conditions as prescribed byAct.
(4) When the President has proclaimed martial law, he shall notify the National Assembly without delay.
(5) When the National Assembly requests the lifting of martial law with the concurrent vote of a majority of the total members of the National Assembly, the President shall comply.

Article 78

The President shall appoint and dismiss public officials under the conditions as prescribed by the Constitution and by Act.

Article 79

(1) The President may grant amnesty, commutation, and restoration of rights under the conditions as prescribed by Act.
(2) The President shall receive the consent of the National Assembly in granting a general amnesty.
(3) Matters pertaining to amnesty, commutation, and restoration of rights shall be determined by Act.

Article 80

The President shall award decorations and other honors under the conditions as prescribed by Act.

Article 81

The President may appear before and address the National Assembly or express his views by written message.

Article 82

The acts of the President under law shall be executed in writing, and such documents shall be countersigned by the Prime Minister and the members of the State Council concerned. The same shall apply to military affairs.

Article 83

The President shall not concurrently hold the office of Prime Minister, a membership in the State Council, the head of any Executive Ministry, nor other public or private posts as prescribed by Act.

Article 84

The President shall not be charged with a criminal offense during his tenure of office except for insurrection or treason.

Article 85

Matters pertaining to the status and courteous treatment of former Presidents shall be determined by Act.

SECTION 2 The Executive Branch

SUB-SECTION 1 The Prime Minister and Members of the State Council

Article 86

(1) The Prime Minister shall be appointed by the President with the consent of the National Assembly.

(2) The Prime Minister shall assist the President and shall direct the Executive Ministries under order of the President.

(3) No member of the military shall be appointed Prime Minister unless he is retired from active duty.

Article 87

(1) The members of the State Council shall be appointed by the President on the recommendation of the Prime Minister.

(2) The members of the State Council shall assist the President in the conduct of State affairs and as constituents of the State Council, shall deliberate on State affairs.
(3) The Prime Minister may recommend to the President the removal of a member of the State Council from office.
(4) No member of the military shall be appointed a member of the State Council unless he is retired from active duty.

SUB-SECTION 2 The State Council

Article 88
(1) The State Council shall deliberate on important policies that fall within the power of the Executive.
(2) The State Council shall be composed of the President, the Prime Minister, and other members whose number shall not be more than thirty and not less than fifteen.
(3) The President shall be the chairman of the State Council, and the Prime Minister shall be the Vice-Chairman.
Article 89
The following matters shall be referred to the State Council for deliberation:
1. Basic plans for state affairs and general policies of the Executive;
2. Declaration of war, conclusion of peace, and other important matters pertaining to foreign policy;
3. Draft amendments to the Constitution, proposals for national referendums, proposed treaties, legislative bills, and proposed presidential decrees;
4. Budgets, settlement of accounts, basic plans for disposal of state properties, contracts incurring financial obligation on the State, and other important financial matters;

5. Emergency orders and emergency financial and economic actions or orders by the President, and declaration and termination of martial law;
6. Important military affairs;
7. Requests for convening an extraordinary session of the National Assembly;
8. Awarding of honors;
9. Granting of amnesty, commutation, and restoration of rights;
10. Demarcation of jurisdiction between Executive Ministries;
11. Basic plans concerning delegation or allocation of powers within the Executive;
12. Evaluation and analysis of the administration of State affairs;
13. Formulation and coordination of important policies of each Executive Ministry;
14. Action for the dissolution of a political party;
15. Examination of petitions pertaining to executive policies submitted or referred to the Executive;
16. Appointment of the Prosecutor General, the Chairman of the Joint Chiefs of Staff, the Chief of Staff of each armed service, the presidents of national universities, ambassadors, and such other public officials and managers of important State-run enterprises as designated by Act; and
17. Other matters presented by the President, the Prime Minister or a member of the State Council.

Article 90

(1) An Advisory Council of Elder Statesmen, composed of elder statesmen, may be established to advise the President on important affairs of State.
(2) The immediate former President shall become the Chairman of the Advisory Council of Elder Statesmen. Provided, that if there is no immediate former President, the President shall appoint the Chairman.

(3) The organization, function, and other necessary matters pertaining to the Advisory Council of Elder Statesmen shall be determined by Act.

Article 91

(1) A National Security Council shall be established to advise the President on the formulation of foreign, military, and domestic policies related to national security prior to their deliberation by the State Council.

(2) The meetings of the National Security Council shall be presided over by the President.

(3) The organization, function, and other necessary matters pertaining to the National Security Council shall be determined by Act.

Article 92

(1) An Advisory Council on Democratic and Peaceful Unification may be established to advise the President on the formulation of peaceful unification policies.

(2) The organization, function, and other necessary matters pertaining to the Advisory Council on Democratic and Peaceful Unification shall be determined by Act.

Article 93

(1) A National Economic Advisory Council may be established to advise the President on the formulation of important policies for developing the national economy.

(2) The organization, function, and other necessary matters pertaining to the National Economic Advisory Council shall be determined by Act.

SUB-SECTION 3 The Executive Ministries

Article 94

Heads of Executive Ministries shall be appointed by the President from among members of the State Council on the recommendation of the Prime Minister.

Article 95

The Prime Minister or the head of each Executive Ministry may, under the powers delegated by Act or Presidential Decree or ex officio, issue ordinances of the Prime Minister or the Executive Ministry concerning matters that are within their jurisdiction.

Article 96

The establishment, organization, and function of each Executive Ministry shall be determined by Act.

SUB-SECTION 4 The Board of Audit and Inspection

Article 97

The Board of Audit and Inspection shall be established under the direct supervision of the President to inspect and examine the settlement of the revenues and expenditures of the State, the accounts of the State and other organizations specified by Act and the job performances of the executive agencies and public officials.

Article 98

(1) The Board of Audit and Inspection shall be composed of not less than five and not more than eleven members, including the Chairman.

(2) The Chairman of the Board shall be appointed by the President with the consent of the National Assembly. The term of office of the Chairman shall be four years and he may be reappointed only once.

(3) The members of the Board shall be appointed by the President on the recommendation of the Chairman. The term of office of the members shall be four years and they may be reappointed only once.

Article 99

The Board of Audit and Inspection shall inspect the closing of accounts of revenues and expenditures each year and report the results to the President and the National Assembly in the following year.

Article 100

The organization and function of the Board of Audit and Inspection, the qualifications of its members, the range of the public officials subject to inspection, and other necessary matters shall be determined by Act.

CHAPTER V THE COURTS

Article 101

(1) Judicial power shall be vested in courts composed of judges.

(2) The courts shall be composed of the Supreme Court, which is the highest court of the State, and other courts at specified levels.

(3) Qualifications for judges shall be determined by Act.

Article 102

(1) Departments may be established in the Supreme Court.

(2) There shall be Supreme Court Justices at the Supreme Court. Provided, that judges other than Supreme Court Justices may be assigned to the Supreme Court under the conditions as prescribed by Act.

(3) The organization of the Supreme Court and lower courts shall be determined by Act.

Article 103

Judges shall rule independently according to their conscience and in conformity with the Constitution and laws.

Article 104

(1) The Chief Justice of the Supreme Court shall be appointed by the

President with the consent of the National Assembly.

(2) The Supreme Court Justices shall be appointed by the President on the recommendation of the Chief Justice and with the consent of the National Assembly.

(3) Judges other than the Chief Justice and the Supreme Court Justices shall be appointed by the Chief Justice with the consent of the Conference of Supreme Court Justices.

Article 105

(1) The term of office of the Chief justice shall be six years, without reappointment.

(2) The term of office of the Justices of the Supreme Court shall be six years and they may be reappointed as prescribed by Act.

(3) The term of office of judges other than the Chief Justice and Justices of the Supreme Court shall be ten years and they may be reappointed under the conditions as prescribed by Act.

(4) The retirement age of judges shall be determined by Act.

Article 106

(1) No judge shall be removed from office except by impeachment or a sentence of imprisonment without prison labor or heavier punishment, nor shall he be suspended from office, have his salary reduced, or suffer any other unfavorable treatment except by disciplinary action.

(2) In the event a judge is unable to discharge his official duties because of serious mental or physical impairment, he may be retired from office under the conditions as prescribed by Act.

Article 107

(1) When the constitutionality of a law is at issue in a trial, the court shall request a decision of the Constitutional Court, and shall judge according to the decision thereof.

(2) The Supreme Court shall have the power to make a final review of the constitutionality or legality of administrative decrees, regulations or actions, when their constitutionality or legality is at issue in a trial.

(3) Administrative appeals may be conducted as a procedure prior to a judicial trial. The procedure of administrative appeals shall be determined by Act and shall be in conformity with the principles of judicial procedures.

Article 108

The Supreme Court may establish, within the scope of an Act, regulations pertaining to judicial proceedings and internal discipline and regulations on administrative matters of the court.

Article 109

Trials and decisions of the courts shall be open to the public. Provided, that when there is a danger that such trials may undermine the national security or disturb public safety and order, or be harmful to public morals, trials may be closed to the public by court decision.

Article 110

(1) Courts-martial may be established as special courts to exercise jurisdiction over military trials.

(2) The Supreme Court shall have the final appellate jurisdiction over courts-martial.

(3) The organization and authority of courts-martial and the qualifications of their judges shall be determined by Act.

(4) Military trials under an extraordinary martial law may not be appealed in case of crimes of soldiers and employees of the military; military espionage; and crimes as defined by Act in regard to sentinels, sentry posts, supply of harmful foods and beverages, and prisoners of war, except in the case of a death sentence.

CHAPTER Ⅵ THE CONSTITUTIONAL COURT

Article 111

(1) The Constitutional Court shall have jurisdiction over the following matters:

1. The constitutionality of a law upon the request of the courts;
2. Impeachment;
3. Dissolution of a political party;
4. Competence disputes between State agencies, between State agencies and local governments, and between local governments; and
5. Constitutional complaint as prescribed by Act.

(2) The Constitutional Court shall be composed of nine Justices qualified to be court judges, and they shall be appointed by the President.

(3) Among the Justices referred to in paragraph (2), three shall be appointed from persons selected by the National Assembly, and three shall be appointed from persons nominated by the Chief Justice of the Supreme Court.

(4) The president of the Constitutional Court shall be appointed by the President from among the Justices with the consent of the National Assembly.

Article 112

(1) The term of office of the Justices of the Constitutional Court shall be six years and they may be reappointed under the conditions as prescribed by Act.

(2) The Justices of the Constitutional Court shall not join any political party, nor shall they participate in political activities.

(3) No Justice of the Constitutional Court shall be expelled from office except by impeachment or a sentence of imprisonment without prison labor or heavier punishment.

Article 113

(1) When the Constitutional Court makes a decision on the constitutionality of a law, a decision of impeachment, a decision of dissolution of a political party, or an affirmative decision regarding the constitutional complaint, the concurrence of six Justices or more shall be required.

(2) The Constitutional Court may establish regulations relating to its proceedings and internal discipline and regulations on administrative matters within the limits of Act.

(3) The organization, function, and other necessary matters of the Constitutional Court shall be determined by Act.

CHAPTER Ⅶ ELECTION MANAGEMENT

Article 114

(1) Election commissions shall be established for the purpose of fair management of elections and national referenda, and dealing with administrative affairs concerning political parties.

(2) The National Election Commission shall be composed of three members appointed by the President, three members selected by the National Assembly, and three members designated by the Chief Justice of the Supreme Court. The Chairman of the Commission shall be elected from among the members.

(3) The term of office of the members of the Commission shall be six years.

(4) The members of the Commission shall not join political parties nor shall they participate in political activities.

(5) No member of the Commission shall be expelled from office except by impeachment or a sentence of imprisonment without prison labor or heavier punishment.

(6) The National Election Commission may establish, within the limit of Acts and decrees, regulations relating to the management of elections, national referenda, and administrative affairs concerning political parties and may also establish regulations relating to internal discipline that are compatible with Act.
(7) The organization, function, and other necessary matters of the election commissions at each level shall be determined by Act.

Article 115

(1) Election commissions at each level may issue necessary instructions to administrative agencies concerned with respect to administrative affairs pertaining to elections and national referenda such as the preparation of the poll books.
(2) Administrative agencies concerned, upon receipt of such instructions, shall comply.

Article 116

(1) Election campaigns shall be conducted under the management of the election commissions at each level within the limit set by Act. Equal opportunity shall be guaranteed.
(2) Except as otherwise prescribed by Act, expenditures for elections shall not be imposed on political parties or candidates.

CHAPTER Ⅷ LOCAL AUTONOMY

Article 117

(1) Local governments shall deal with administrative matters pertaining to the welfare of local residents, manage properties, and may enact provisions relating to local autonomy, within the limit of Acts and subordinate statutes.
(2) The types of local governments shall be determined by Act.

Article 118

(1) A local government shall have a council.

(2) The organization and powers of local councils, and the election of members; election procedures for heads of local governments; and other matters pertaining to the organization and operation of local governments shall be determined by Act.

CHAPTER Ⅸ THE ECONOMY

Article 119

(1) The economic order of the Republic of Korea shall be based on a respect for the freedom and creative initiative of enterprises and individuals in economic affairs.

(2) The State may regulate and coordinate economic affairs in order to maintain the balanced growth and stability of the national economy, to ensure proper distribution of income, to prevent the domination of the market and the abuse of economic power and to democratize the economy through harmony among the economic agents.

Article 120

(1) Licenses to exploit, develop, or utilize minerals and all other important underground resources, marine resources, water power, and natural powers available for economic use may be granted for a period of time under the conditions as prescribed by Act.

(2) The land and natural resources shall be protected by the State, and the State shall establish a plan necessary for their balanced development and utilization.

Article 121

(1) The State shall endeavor to realize the land-to-the-tillers principle with

respect to agricultural land. Tenant farming shall be prohibited.

(2) The leasing of agricultural land and the consignment management of agricultural land to increase agricultural productivity and to ensure the rational utilization of agricultural land or due to unavoidable circumstances, shall be recognized under the conditions prescribed by Act.

Article 122

The State may impose, under the conditions prescribed by Act, restrictions or obligations necessary for the efficient and balanced utilization, development, and preservation of the land of the nation that is the basis for the productive activities and daily lives of all citizens.

Article 123

(1) The State shall establish and implement a plan to comprehensively develop and support the farm and fishing communities in order to protect and foster agriculture and fisheries.

(2) The State shall have the duty to foster regional economies to ensure the balanced development of all regions.

(3) The State shall protect and foster small and medium enterprises.

(4) In order to protect the interests of farmers and fishermen, the State shall endeavor to stabilize the prices of agricultural and fishery products by maintaining an equilibrium between the demand and supply of such products and improving their marketing and distribution systems.

(5) The State shall foster organizations founded on the spirit of self-help among farmers, fishermen, and businessmen engaged in small and medium industry and shall guarantee their independent activities and development.

Article 124

The State shall guarantee the consumer protection movement intended to encourage sound consumption activities and improvement in the quality of products under the conditions as prescribed by Act.

Article 125

The State shall foster foreign trade, and may regulate and coordinate it.

Article 126

Private enterprises shall not be nationalized nor transferred to ownership by a local government, nor shall their management be controlled or administered by the State, except in cases as prescribed by Act, to meet urgent necessities of national defense or the national economy.

Article 127

(1) The State shall strive to develop the national economy by developing science and technology, information and human resources and encouraging innovation.

(2) The State shall establish a system of national standards. (3)The President may establish advisory organizations necessary to achieve the purpose referred to in paragraph (1).

CHAPTER X AMENDMENTS TO THE CONSTITUTION

Article 128

(1) A proposal to amend the Constitution shall be introduced either by a majority of the total members of the National Assembly or by the President.

(2) Amendments to the Constitution for the extension of the term of office of the President or for a change allowing for the reelection of the President shall not be effective for the President in office at the time of the proposal for such amendments to the Constitution.

Article 129

Proposed amendments to the Constitution shall be put before the public by the President for twenty days or more.

Article 130

(1) The National Assembly shall decide upon the proposed amendments within sixty days of the public announcement, and passage by the National Assembly shall require the concurrent vote of two thirds or more of the total members of the National Assembly.

(2) The proposed amendments to the Constitution shall be submitted to a national referendum not later than thirty days after the passage by the National Assembly, and shall be determined by more than one half of all votes cast by more than one half of voters eligible to vote in elections for members of the National Assembly.

(3) When the proposed amendments to the Constitution receive the concurrence prescribed in paragraph (2), the amendments to the Constitution shall be finalized, and the President shall promulgate it without delay.

ADDENDA

Article 1

This Constitution shall enter into force on the twenty-fifth day of February, anno Domini Nineteen hundred and eighty-eight. Provided, that the enactment or amendment of Acts necessary to implement this Constitution, the elections of the President and the National Assembly under this Constitution and other preparations to implement this Constitution may be carried out prior to the entry into force of this Constitution.

Article 2

(1) The first presidential election under this Constitution shall be held not later than forty days before this Constitution enters into force.

(2) The term of office of the first President under this Constitution shall commence on the date of its enforcement.

Article 3

(1) The first elections of the National Assembly under this Constitution shall be held within six months from the promulgation of this Constitution. The term of office of the members of the first National Assembly elected under this Constitution shall commence on the date of the first convening of the National Assembly under this Constitution.

(2) The term of office of the members of the National Assembly incumbent at the time this Constitution is promulgated shall terminate the day prior to the first convening of the National Assembly under paragraph (1).

Article 4

(1) Public officials and officers of enterprises appointed by the Government, who are in office at the time of the enforcement of this Constitution, shall be considered as having been appointed under this Constitution. Provided, that public officials whose election procedures or appointing authorities are

changed under this Constitution, the Chief Justice of the Supreme Court and the Chairman of the Board of Audit and Inspection shall remain in office until such time as their successors are chosen under this Constitution, and their terms of office shall terminate the day before the installation of their successors.

(2) Judges attached to the Supreme Court who is not the Chief Justice, Justices of the Supreme Court, and other judges and justices who are in office at the time of the enforcement of this Constitution shall be considered as having been appointed under this Constitution notwithstanding the proviso of paragraph (1).

(3) Those provisions of this Constitution which prescribe the terms of office of public officials or which restrict the number of terms that public officials may serve, shall take effect upon the dates of the first elections or the first appointments of such public officials under this Constitution.

Article 5

Acts, decrees, ordinances, and treaties in force at the time this Constitution enters into force, shall remain valid unless they are contrary to this Constitution.

Article 6

Those organizations existing at the time of the enforcement of this Constitution which have been performing the functions falling within the authority of new organizations to be created under this Constitution, shall continue to exist and perform such functions until such time as the new organizations are created under this Constitution.

Index

Kag-Keun Yu

- Professor, College of Law, Sun-Moon University
- Ph.D. in Law, Hiroshima National University, Japan
- Professor, College of Law, Han-Nam University
- Visiting Professor, College of Law, Chuo University, Japan
- Member, Chung-Nam Labor Relations Tribunal
- Policy Consultant, Ministry of Employment and Labor
- Director, Korean Society of Labor Law
- Vice-Chairman, Korean Society of Comparative Labor Law
- Member, Panel of Examiners for National Bar Examination and for the Highest Civil Service Examination

Bibliography

- Understanding of Law (2011)
- Labor Law 1, 2 (2009)
- The Case Study of Labor Law (2010), etc.

유 각 근

- 선문대학교 법과대학 교수
- 법학박사(일본히로시마대학교 대학원 법학전공 졸업)
- 한남대학교 법과대학 교수
- 일본 중앙대학 법학부 객원교수
- 충남노동위원회 심판공익위원
- 고용노동부 정책자문위원
- 한국노동법학회 이사
- 한국비교노동법학회 부회장
- 사법시험 및 행정고시 시험출제위원

저서

- 법학의 이해(2011)
- 노동법 연습(2010)
- 노동법1,2(2009) 등

In-Hee Kwon

- Associate Professor
- Department of Law, College of Law, Sun Moon University, Korea

Received

- B.S. in Physics, Yonsei University, Korea
- Ph.D. in Physics, Iowa State University, USA
- M.A. in Law, Chungnam National University, Korea

Completed

- Legal English for Practitioners, CELOP, Boston University
- General Course on Intellectual Property, WIPO Worldwide Academy, WIPO
- Key Doctrines in American Law and US Legal Practice, Summer Legal Institute in London, School of Law, Boston University

Hold

- License for Patent Attorney

권 인 희

선문대학교 법과대학 법학과 부교수, 변리사

- 연세대학교 이과대학 물리학과 졸업 (이학사)
- 미국 아이오와주립대학교 대학원 물리학과 졸업 (이학박사)
- 충남대학교 대학원 법학과 졸업 (법학석사)

- 보스톤대학교 실무자를 위한 법률영어과정 수료
- 세계지적재산권기구 지적재산권 일반교육과정 수료
- 보스톤대학교 런던여름학교 미국법과정 수료

Basic Legal English

By Kag-Keun Yu and In-Hee Kwon

초판 인쇄 | August 25, 2011
초판 발행 | August 27, 2011

펴낸곳 | Sun-Moon University
100, Kalsan-ri, Tangjeong-myeon, Asan-si, Chung Nam, Korea
Tel 041-530-2827, Fax 041-530-2979
등록 | September 25, 1998(No 9)
펴낸이 | Bong-Tea Kim

ISBN | 978-89-8423-696-7 정가 25,000원